ABOUT *A PAINFUL DUTY*
FORTY YEARS AT THE CRIMINAL BAR
"Very rarely have I read a memoir or
autobiography whose author had as
overwhelming concern for truth and
fairness as Evans displays in this book."
— Alex Rettie, *Alberta Views*

ABOUT *5000 DEAD DUCKS*
LUST AND REVOLUTION IN THE OILSANDS
"5000 Dead Ducks may be a satire,
a fever dream of sorts, but its message is clear:
When it comes to the oilsands, the stakes are
so high that anything is possible."
— Gillian Steward, *The Toronto Star*

ABOUT *TOUGH CRIMES*
TRUE CASES BY TOP CANADIAN CRIMINAL LAWYERS
"Incredible collection of memorable cases ... Readers
go behind the scenes as lawyers prepare for difficult
cases and see how they handle their clients, witnesses,
and other evidence during and after trial."
— Daryl Slade, *The Calgary Herald*

LESS
PAINFUL
DUTIES

Reflections on the
Revolution in the
Legal Profession

Other Books by C.D. Evans

A Painful Duty: Forty Years at the Criminal Bar

Milt Harradence: The Western Flair

Matthew's Passion

with Lorene Shyba

5000 Dead Ducks: Lust and Revolution in the Oilsands

*Tough Crimes: True Cases by
Top Canadian Criminal Lawyers*

LESS PAINFUL DUTIES

*Reflections on the
Revolution in the
Legal Profession*

C.D. EVANS

DURVILE
PUBLICATIONS

Durvile Publications Ltd.

Calgary, Alberta, Canada
www.durvile.com
Copyright © 2017 Durvile Publications Ltd.

NATIONAL LIBRARY OF CANADA
CATALOGUING IN PUBLICATIONS DATA
Evans, Christopher Dudley

Less Painful Duties: Reflections on the Revolution in the Legal Profession
Issued in print and electronic formats
ISBN: 978-0-9952322-1-1 (print pbk) ISBN: 978-0-9952322-0-4 (epub)
ISBN: 978-1-988824-01-7 (audiobook)

1. Biography
2. Canadian Law
3. Criminal Law

I. Evans, C.D.

Book Two in the Reflections Series

We would like to acknowledge the support of the
Alberta Government through the Alberta Book Fund.
Printed by Houghton Boston Printers, Saskatoon, Saskatchewan.
Durvile is a member of the Book Publishers Association of Alberta (BPAA)
and Association of Canadian Publishers (ACP)

First edition, first printing. 2017

Dedicated to my learned friends and professional colleagues with whom I shared the revolution.

And to Patrick Fagan QC, Clayton Rice QC, Kaysi Fagan and Sean Fagan, whose generosity keeps the old man in touch with his Profession.

Table of Contents

INTRODUCTION

Let me begin at the end. The aging process is instructive, and at times corrosive. I suppose at age three score years and seventeen, I am spiraling down inexorably to the final boarding process, inevitably to be either warehoused drooling and incontinent, or dead.

This is therefore an appropriate occasion for reflections about significant events/years in one's life and career and in particular the revolution in my Profession. I planned on including as Part 2 accounts of individuals whom one admired and emulated, liked, or – in some cases – roundly disliked; and publishing the recordings of erudite witnesses who also chose to contribute their professional experiences to my book. But I was a witness to a true revolution, and I have subordinated all other considerations to recording and reflecting upon the radical changes that occurred in the legal profession in this country over the 50 years of my law practice.

In that period of time when I was contemplating the successor to my 2010 memoir *A Painful Duty: Forty Years at the Criminal Bar*, I cannot overplay the significance of finding quite by happenstance a copy of the December 30, 1989 edition of *The Globe and Mail* newspaper, inexplicably wrapped in plastic on the bottom shelf of the bathroom closet at my mountain retreat. This edition was essentially a compendium of the important events, political, social and cultural, of the tumultuous era of the 1980s. Gorbachev and Reagan dominated world affairs reportage, but the repatriation of the Canadian Constitution in 1982 was a major feature. I was particularly taken by four articles in which the writers looked back over some stunning events on the Canadian scene in that past decade. What sat me up

1

me up right there was that it was in the 1980s that some of the really revolutionary events in society and in my Profession came about, and it was in this decade's crucible that the wheels of change began to move forward, then roll on of their own accord. The four articles that I actually clipped dealt with: 1. 'The Charter of Rights'; 2. 'The emergence of Women from male misogyny, dominance and dictatorship'; 3. 'The computer'; 4. 'Canadian crimes of passion'. These four articles all contributed to exploding the myth that Canada was a backward and somewhat second-rate place where peasants toiled in the mines and fished and hauled wood and water and guarded the horned cattle on the hill. And these well-researched surveys set the stage for my own reflections on the revolution that had occurred over fifty years within my Profession.

I have tried as a chronicler to obey the admonitions of the late Chairman Mao: "Be united, alert, earnest and lively," but some of what I feel obliged to say may present as pedestrian and plodding. Well, it's the song, not the singer.

The great joy of producing this book is this context: after I had declared a pox on my Profession, my Profession took me back. There was an interregnum of seven years. My reason for going on the inactive list in 2005 was not to rest, but to write books, and I did. I also thought that after forty years engaged in combat I had come to the end of my use to my Profession, and that as the mental and physical faculties diminished I should go into inexorable decline. This is the cold hand that grips the gunfighter as he realizes that his eye is getting dim and his arm is becoming stiff and slow, and that there is always someone who is faster. I confess I once reveled in my response to a young and keen law student who attended the advanced advocacy course taught by me and my long-term nemesis turned law partner, Peter Martin QC: "Who's the faster gun, you or Mr. Martin?" I replied, actually I borrowed the line from Milt Harradence, "You wouldn't want to bet your life on the difference." But that was then.

In May 1999, determined to write more and practice less, I reluctantly severed my connection with my old firm and fetched up in the decayed elegance of the Grain Exchange Building in Calgary, circa

1909, with the emphasis on 'decayed'.

As it turned out, it was as well that I started to back off law practice, eventually going voluntarily on the inactive list of the Law Society in March 2005, as the illness afflicting my late beloved wife intensified in its severity and I found myself more and more in the role of the caregiver. I hasten to add that she would have done the same and more for me, in spades, such was our loving relationship. She was my soulmate in all things instant. So I basically finished up the few files I had, mainly cops who found themselves in trouble with the law or the disciplinary processes of the Calgary Police Service or the RCMP, and led for the plaintiff Crown Prosecutor in the major case *Krieger v. Law Society of Alberta*, which I discussed at some length in my preceding memoir, *A Painful Duty*.

My beloved wife Bernice died in October 2009. As with all grieving widowers, I was devastated by her loss and retreated into what can only be described as a dissociative state. I first sought solace in reclusivity, socked away in my mountain fiefdom with strong drink, sad music, exhaustive disturbed sleep.

What pulled me up by my bootstraps, as opposed to being hoisted on my own petard, was to get to work on my memoir of forty years of practice at the Criminal Bar, *A Painful Duty*. Most people have not the slightest inkling of what it takes to write a book, to actually sit down and churn out chapter after chapter draft, and then to suffer the slings and arrows of a hard-boiled but highly competent editor. Thus the better part of 2010 was taken up with this toil, and the result was a handsome book edited and designed by my close friend and business partner, Dr. Lorene Shyba. The book was well received by my Profession and at large by the public, and was enthusiastically endorsed by the Legal Archives Society of Alberta who had me as their featured speaker at the sell-out historical dinners in Edmonton and Calgary of 2010.

It had not been my intention to write the sequel so quickly. The judicious editing of my Memoir inevitably resulted in a number of chapters hitting the cutting room floor, some of which should stay there and some of which have been resurrected for this tome. The passage of events went something like this: the following year, Dr. Shyba and I co-wrote a novel, *5000 Dead Ducks: Lust and Revolution in the Oilsands*, which we knew to be a sure winner in sales and to which the public response was underwhelming. Of course the problem was obvious: for one to write a satire taking the mickey out of politicians and oil sands entrepreneurs in this province would be the kiss of death, and that's how it turned out. The greater public, dependent upon the obscene revenues generated by the oil sands, shrunk from our book like Count Dracula from the crucifix.

With *5000 Dead Ducks* launched, with all the accompanying trials and tribulations of distribution and marketing, we cast about for a further suitable project for Durance Vile Publications (the company now know as Durvile Publications, since its transfer to Dr. Shyba), and in due course decided upon *Tough Crimes*. The object was to approach the top criminal lawyers in Canada, my friends and professional colleagues for decades now at the top of their Profession, and invite them to contribute their personal account of a case that they had found particularly disquieting or disturbing. This concept was received quite enthusiastically by those we approached, some thirty in number, and indeed Dr. Shyba and I expended a lot of time and treasure attempting to put this book together. The problem was to get obviously heavily engaged criminal lawyers and judges to take the time to write 3,500 or so words. After we had advanced the deadline three times, and indulged in a deal of whip-and-carrot cajoling, we found ourselves with nineteen really first-rate contributions, and a solid book.

The nineteen criminal lawyers and judges who contributed, including myself, wrote about a case she or he conducted either as prosecutor or defence lawyer that we had found disquieting and that still haunted us. The Hon. John Major, CC, QC, retired Justice of the Supreme Court of Canada, in his jacket introduction stated: "Tough Crimes demonstrates that Crown prosecutors and criminal defence lawyers do not escape unscathed from serious trials. The disturbing memories remain."

As to disturbing memories, the quietly eloquent British poet

Philip Larkin, writing to his friend the novelist Barbara Pym, July 1971, observed:

> Has anyone ever done any work on why memories are always unhappy? ... sudden stabbing memories of especially absurd or painful moments that one is suffused and excoriated by; ... I suppose if one lives to be old, one's entire waking life will be spent turning on the spit of recollection over the fires of mingled shame, pain or remorse. Cheerful prospect!

As it turned out, *Tough Crimes* was an extraordinary success. We launched it at the Danish Canadian Club on November 13, 2014, which was exactly fifty years from the day I was Called to the Bar. It has, since the launch, sold across Canada over four thousand copies, and is now in a third printing. Which simply illustrates that nonfiction does better than fiction.

About the time that I was immersing myself in the writing and publishing field, I received a call from my old law associate Patrick Fagan QC. Fagan had been an exemplary RCMP cop for some ten years while raising a family of five children. He was and is a superior man, of every kidney. He completed his bachelor of arts with distinction while working a full shift as an RCMP officer and looking after his family; after ten years, he petitioned the Force to send him to law school, and they refused (i) as "the quota had been filled", and (ii) the RCMP neglect their best and brightest. Patrick therefore resigned from the Force with honour, attended the University of Western Ontario law school, and graduated a gold medalist. He spent some five years in the wilderness of a large firm, where he became a most valuable associate, and then set up his own practice of criminal law. At once, I worked with Pat, retaining him as my junior and later co-counsel on a number of significant cases in which we achieved significant results. In or about 2011 - 2012, Pat and his associate Ian McKay approached me generously to join their Firm, and that is exactly what I did. Thus Evans Fagan McKay, later Evans Fagan Rice McKay, when the distinguished lawyer and legal scholar Clayton Rice QC joined us.

I had to petition the Law Society for readmission to active membership, having been on the inactive list for some seven years. The great fear I had was having to write Donald Goodfellow's builders lien exam! I had to fill out multiple forms for the Law Society bureaucrats, among them excruciating detail on what I had done in the intervening seven years "to stay in touch with my Profession." This was not very hard: in addition to being appointed the literary executor of the estate of the late John Wesley McClung, Senior Justice of Appeal, I spoke at several legal functions; wrote the introduction to the Law Society of Alberta 100th anniversary book together with a number of articles for it which were also published; wrote my own memoir *A Painful Duty: Forty Years at the Criminal Bar*; and I was asked by the Legal Education Society of Alberta to take part as faculty in their Advanced Advocacy course. So the bottom line is that they let me back to practice on my undertaking to restrict my practice to criminal law and appellate advocacy, which I was more than happy to do.

Thus I returned to combat, and the once born-again Bencher became the born-again barrister, to the great amusement of many of my contemporaries. I have not ruled out a subliminal desire to continually reinvent myself.

Of course, in leaving the practice of law and resolving never to return – in print – then seven years later going back to active practice, the born-again barrister; as well as not running again for the Benchers after three two-year terms, and four years later running again, the born-again Bencher, I was accused of inconsistency. But one can always fall back on Emerson: "A foolish consistency is the hobgoblin of little minds!"

I particularly recall a mentor and close friend rebuking me with the criticism, not unfounded, "You are impulsive." To which one may respond with Thomas Cromwell, courtesy of Hilary Mantell in *Wolf Hall*: "If you are without impulses, you are, to a degree, without joy."

I was Called to the Bar in November 1964. I went inactive from 2005 to 2012, returned to the active practicing list in 2012, and finally packed it in at the end of 2015, coming on fifty-one years a lawyer. At the generous invitation of my Firm, Evans Fagan & Rice, I have maintained my association with my Profession and my office on the Firm premises in the company of my esteemed colleagues. I had remained an inactive member of the Law Society in the 2005 to 2012 interregnum, and was therefore still a member so far as I was concerned, but the Law Society has not honoured my contributions to my Profession with the standard fifty-year certificate. Well, that's the village.

My intent in this Memoir is to discuss the phenomenon of the revolutions in our Profession upon which I found myself at the cusp. It was indeed a revolutionary fifty-year period in Canadian legal history: the Female ascendancy, the Charter of Rights, legal aid, prosecutorial disclosure, governing bodies, judicial appointments, the computer and the cellphone, social media. I shall therefore have to relinquish the pleasure of discussing "learned friends and some not so learned and not so friendly."

My friends, colleagues and associates are aware that I am a big fan of the late Edmund Burke. Burke is said to be "the first Tory" and he, philosophically, plainly was. In Burke's time, it was very fashionable to be extremely right-wing, but he was not hidebound by the party line, and was famous for speaking out on unpopular causes. Example: Burke was much against Lord North's determined prosecution of the war against the American colonists, speaking eloquently in the House on the fact that it would be far more appropriate to negotiate with the 'rebels', who were not rebels but who were Englishmen like themselves. Give them a voice in Parliament, he said. He was belittled for his pains.

Burke was a great supporter of the American colonists, but he was also a conservative traditionalist, believing in the value of 'inheritance', and he did not view the French Revolution with the same equanimity.

I have been plowing through Edmund Burke's *Reflections on the Revolution in France*, reading it back-to-back with Thomas Paine's *Rights of Man*. Thomas Paine, in his *Rights of Man*, sought to refute Burke. What is significant for all barristers is the fact that Paine was charged with treason in England for the very crime of writing and distributing this treatise. It was certainly not fair that Paine was prosecuted for having the temerity to write his eloquent response to Burke's chastisement of a young member of the new French revolutionary National Assembly, but the truly profound impact of his trial was the legacy gifted to our Profession by Thomas Erskine KC, the leading barrister of the day. Erskine undertook Paine's defence, notwithstanding that it cost him the office of Attorney General of England, and held him up to vilification, ridicule and abuse from several quarters, including parliamentarians and nobility. He never regretted this, stating that it was of no moment in contrast to the necessity to do his duty to defend Paine. He insisted on undertaking the brief upon being requested to do so by Paine, and in his memorable address to the jury in Paine's case he delivered the most famous admonition in the history of the Bar that should be force-fed to every first-year law student showing an interest in trial advocacy, and which does not stale with repetition.

Erskine did not call evidence, admitted that Paine had written the *Rights of Man*, and instead chose to address the jury. He opened with his famous admonition:

> I will for ever, at all hazards, assert the dignity, independence and integrity of the English Bar, without which impartial justice, the most valuable part of the English Constitution, can have no existence. From the moment that any advocate can be permitted to say that he will, or will not, stand between the Crown and the subject arraigned in the court where he daily sits to practise, from that moment the liberties of England are at an end. If the advocate refuses to defend, from what he may think of the charge or of the defence, he assumes the character of the Judge; nay, he assumes it before the hour of judgment; and in proportion to his rank and reputation, puts the heavy influence of, perhaps, a mistaken opinion into the scales against the accused, in whose favour the benevolent principle of English law makes all presumptions.

The true Barrister ignores or breaches this admonition at his/her peril. Sadly today, many of our colleagues at the Bar have no concept of what Erskine was articulating, and that is a tragedy for my Profession.

Burke's *Reflections on the Revolution in France* are a much better read than Thomas Carlyle's *The French Revolution*. Hence my choice of the title of this Memoir, which is my overview and final wrap-up of a long hard haul that had its challenges and difficulties, but was always educational and instructive.

• • •

Now fast approaching my seventy-eighth birthday, if I were to be advised by my medical doctors that I had a debilitating, life-threatening, painful and incurable illness, I hope I should be philosophical and adopt Dr. Johnson's axiom: "Nothing concentrates the mind more wonderfully, Sir, than the knowledge that one is to be hanged in two weeks." And endeavor, with concentrated mind, to knock off one more book. In a *National Post* column of January, 2017, the excellent writer Barbara Kay quoted oncologist and bioethicist Ezekiel J. Emanuel, observing that seventy-five "is the age at which he will feel his life is complete and not worth prolonging by artificial means." Dr. Emanuel thinks it an absurd American obsession to madly diet and work out and try thereby to cheat death. At seventy-five years, he plans to stop taking steps in a desperate attempt to prolong life: no more colonoscopies, no more cardiac stress tests, no more flu shots, no cancer treatments, no surgery, no dialysis. Only palliative care and medication for pain. That makes a fair bit of sense, although one has to consider that it is not so much the fact of death but the manner of death that is the disturbing preoccupation. Dr. Emanuel is concerned that his creativity would diminish with age. That is a major consideration. If I do not get a premonition that my independent memory and my mind are slipping away into dementia, hopefully friends will be able to apprise me of this fact – "A very interesting story, CD, but you just told it three times" – and I shall take myself off to the euthanasia center. If the body quits, well, one can still stagger around. If the mind gives up, it's all over.

Even at seventy-seven years, I am reluctant to shuffle off this mortal coil. But there are days that I do chafe at this vale of tears, not that as yet I have cause to contemplate leaving this life voluntarily. However, if I feel obliged to do so, I should do so with a minimum of fuss and bother to those for whom I care, e.g. my few friends, my executors, my accountant, my lawyer. In all probability, I shall join a euthanasia club, and when the day comes, simply take a cab one way to the airport, pay the requisite tariff, ask for four fingers of single malt straight up in a white wine glass, a Cuban cigar, and *Bach's Keyboard Concerto in D minor*. Exeunt, and a good way to go, all things considered, better than being warehoused, drooling and incontinent, or passing on in a hospital bed with a tube in every orifice and pseudo-blubbers standing about.

1

ON THE CUSP

It could be said that I had a particularly fortuitous vantage point from which to view the 20th century revolution – a view from the bridge, as it were – not only in my profession but in the world at large. I was born three months after the outbreak of the Second World War. When that unbelievable carnage was concluded, most of Europe and much of the rest of the world lay in ruins, their populations depleted, and Soviet-style communism descended. And it was all over for the class system. I was fortunate in emigrating to Western Canada, but keeping one foot in the old world of my English father. I served in the Canadian armed forces. My maturing years witnessed Korea, the Suez crisis, the liberation of former colonies, the rise of unions, the Cold War and the nuclear race, the Kennedy assassination (I was articling at Macleod Dixon; what were you doing?), The European Union, the ousting of dictators, the advance of prosperous flourishing democracies, the era of immense job creation, "consumer goods and leisure travel, gadgetry, mass spectator sports, and more available housing", the rise of feminism and gay rights, the *Canadian Charter of Rights*, the dismantling of apartheid, space travel, the fall of the Berlin Wall, and the collapse of the Soviet oligarchy. Add to all that the rather negative developments of the Celebrity Adulation Culture and affirmative action.

It is almost impossible for a comfortable Western Canadian, enjoying the benefits of our rights and freedoms handed down literally from the *Magna Carta*, to comprehend the horrendous impact upon humanity of the September 11, 2001 attacks on the World Trade Center. We remain pole-axed by the fallout from the so-called "Arab Spring" turned winter of their discontent.

The Globe and Mail newspaper edition of Dec. 30, 1989 that I have referred to featured a significant article researched and written by Timothy Appleby, reviewing the fundamental societal restructuring by which Canada came into its own dark space as a forum for unspeakable crimes during the 1980s. He writes eloquently of the shock to the nation of the slaughter of fourteen women at Montreal's Ecole polytechnique in the final month of 1989. "In a sense," he reflects, "the killings represented a loss of innocence." As, indeed, other unspeakable crimes in Canada in that decade so horrendously impacted the legal profession and the public: the 1985 bombing of the Air India plane off the coast of Ireland, killing all 329 people aboard; the murder of at least eleven children in British Columbia by Clifford Olsen; other sensational homicides gaining national attention.

Every bit as sobering, the writer reports that Canada was now being pulled into the widening vortex of the criminal drug trade. The lamentable efflorescence of drug crime enriched Canadian defence lawyers, who prospered from the exponential upsurge in this country of all aspects of the narcotics trade as well as the sorts of crimes related to illegal drugs: homicide, robbery, violence. In particular, he notes, cocaine became "the drug of choice for trendy, affluent urbanites." The prominence, pervasiveness, and the size of the illegal drug trade in Canada was in a sense revolutionary, as well as the decision finally taken by the Liberal government in 2017 to legalize marijuana. I deal briefly with this last innovation in a later chapter.

The insertion of the computer and related technology – exponential technology – into every nook and cranny of formerly private lives is nothing short of astounding to our Profession. For the first thirty-five years of my law practice, nobody had a computer and nobody had a cell phone. To say that life was simpler then would be the understatement of all time. These innovations completely revolutionized the former sedate practice of law, the telephone accord, the simple handshake, the courteous letter. Everything now was email and text, and emails and texts formerly thought to be private could be regurgitated and had to be disclosed in litigation. I shall treat of this in some detail, essentially from the point of view of an outsider standing by and watching these things happen so dramatically and so exponentially. From the criminal law context alone, the dominance of *The Canadian Charter of Rights and Freedoms* in all aspects of cell phone and computer seizures by investigating authorities must be filling libraries, if things are still recorded on paper. Every five hundred years, it has been said, a major innovation advances mankind: the wheel, the stirrup, gunpowder, the printing press, electricity, and in our day, the computer. This in turn has spawned the ubiquitous cell phone, instant communication, and the so-called social media networks (which personally I eschew).

We in Alberta were in the front seats of the roller coaster called the oil sands, as oil prices over forty years rose from three dollars to $100 a barrel, and the US percentage of oil from imports moved from twenty percent to sixty percent, now declining sharply. Contrast that, however – speaking of revolutions – with Alberta pitching downward from a 'have' to a 'have-not' province in 2015– 2016, with the precipitous fall in the price of oil per barrel, down as low as $30, and unemployment, commercial and residential foreclosures and vacancies. One reeled from the ousting of the entrenched 'entitlement' Tories and the election – amazement! – of an NDP provincial government.

The New Democratic Party preaches that the meek shall inherit the earth, subject, of course, to a certain amount of estate tax. One of their historical imperatives is that all God's chillun got a robe, and now they want my robe. The sandbagging of the Alberta Tory Party, after more than forty years in power and having become bogged down in a sordid sea of entitlement and preferment, was welcome.

"Democracy," wrote H.L. Menken, "is the theory that the common people know what they want and deserve to get it good and hard." William F. Buckley's telling observation was that it is a fiction that in a free society no fraud can survive for very long after it is publicly discredited. His example is socialism, which is left without serious defenders, but whose forms and manias encroach upon us year after year.

The very suggestion that the NDP would become the government of Alberta is still hard for many Albertans to accept. Their leader, Premier Rachel Notley, whose late father I knew as a well-informed chap who made short work of the ill-informed lightweights who from time to time tried to argue with him, is an excellent first minister who has seen the province through some very hard times. I am confident that the majority of my provincial contemporaries would applaud Premier Notley, particularly when she found herself saddled with the plunge in oil prices and the devastating fire in Fort McMurray.

One nevertheless observes that apparently fused into the collective and individual NDP genetic spiral is their visceral fear of consumerism, capitalism, 'liberal' and 'right wing' governments, climate change deniers, fossil fuels, and militarism. They decry man's 'despoilage' of the planet, hate 'business development', despair at the threat of nuclear obliteration or environmental Armageddon. They love tax-and-spend, and making laws and regulations.

Notwithstanding the ensuing brutal recession, the new socialist government plowed ahead raising taxes, imposing an unwelcome carbon tax, and putting a hard cap on oilsands emissions with the object of limiting future growth in the principal economic engine of the province. Kevin Libin in *The National Post*, Tuesday, February 28, 2017 observed that regular Albertans eschewed these impositions, and were sceptical of global warning alarums or that humans are responsible for climate change.

All that the NDP will do in Alberta after their uncanny election is emphasize the economic gulf between the haves and the have not-leys. "Put the jam on the lower shelf," they cry, "so the little man can have some." They heap coals upon whip-wielding capitalists, big business, US imperialists, cultural invaders, and corporate welfare bums. But I predict that the conglomeration of batty left wingers is not going to last for much longer in right-wing Alberta. The majority of my fellow citizens do not wish to revert to the 12th Century.

• • •

In this thrilling kaleidoscope of massive change, I was part and parcel of the revolution that swept my profession.

And what about our revolution over the past forty years?

I lamented in *A Painful Duty: Forty Years at the Criminal Bar* that I had not left my profession, my profession left me. From my Call to the Bar in 1964, my profession truly underwent five decades of nothing less than a revolution. On balance, I was personally and professionally delighted at some developments and sanguine about others. The negative concomitants are what drove me away from practice, the positive achievements are what brought me back, a born-again barrister. Now, because I can leave at any time, I shall probably hang in, mainly because I enjoy my association with my Profession as an inactive member but still symbolically head up a major criminal law firm, and am not an impotent commentator on the sidelines. The positive rewards of being part of a great Profession probably justified the annual costs and inconveniences and bureaucratic importations of active membership year after year: the license to practice and insurance and the assurance fund, the endless Law Society self-reporting forms, the soporific accounting strictures, the absurd annual requirement to file some sort of a game plan for your personal development as a professional in the coming year, a lot of that surplusage.

As a critic, one speaks from a better podium – not a bully pul- pit, that's for H.M. Judges – as a leader of the Bar than as a retired old fool, sidelined and irrelevant.

I started law practice as an articled student in 1963, and hence was granted a front row seat at all of these events that really shook the hell out of a moribund profession stuck back somewhere at the beginning of the 20th century. Or, as in Calgary, rushing headlong into the 19th century!

I have characterized my role in all of this as being 'on the cusp': I commenced practice with one foot firmly in the old boy network, and the other eagerly seeking a foothold in the new profession. It was possible at times to feel torn, because as sweeping changes engulfed judges and lawyers, much of what I revered about the great traditions and courtesies and civilities of the profession got trampled in the rush.

Seven revolutionary events

The seven truly revolutionary events of the plus fifty years that I have practiced my profession in the mid-to-late 20th century that transformed Canadian lawyers and Law Societies forever are these:

(1) The advent of Legal Aid and Pro Bono *(Chapter 2);*

(2) Law Society governance: the end of the upper middle male / large all-male partner firm dominance of the profession, the Benchers, and the Bench *(Chapter 3);*

(3) The Charter of Rights *(Chapter 4);*

(4) The welcome Female Ascendancy *(Chapter 5);*

(5) Disclosure *(Chapter 6);*

(6) The reconstitution of the Alberta Courts, and Judicial appointments *(Chapter 7);*

(7) The revolutionary impact of the computer and the cell phone, and pervasive social media *(Chapter 8);*

As casualties of the evolution of revolution, two chapters deal respectively with negative concomitants of radical change: The Decline of Advocacy *(Chapter 9);* The changing face of professional camaraderie *(Chapter 10).*

I shall also speak to other revolutionary events in my Profession during the same period, which have both positive and negative aspects. I have combined these in one chapter dealing with Human Rights tribunals; the proposed legalization of drugs; intervenor applications in party and party litigation ; the 'victim' *(Chapter 11).*

These are my personal observations of a legal practitioner immersed, sometimes even overwhelmed, by these revolutionary events. But this is definitely not an academic treatise. I loathe academic books, as I expect do most readers. This book is mercifully free of legal citations, case reports, and similar persiflage. The opinions are my own. If the reader does not like my views, the reader can stop reading this book.

2

LEGAL AID & PRO BONO

Legal Aid was a revolutionary concept. The Alberta Legal Aid Plan, a 1979 joint enterprise of the Law Society and the Provincial Attorney General, ushered in the social-welfare-net era of criminal defence and civil dispute representation. It encapsulated the previous voluntary service to the disadvantaged and marginalized of the Needy Litigant appointment and the traditional request by the Court to counsel to undertake a Dock Brief. The Alberta Legal Aid Plan materially assisted people with legal problems who could not afford to pay for legal services but needed them urgently. The plan also generated some modest fees for struggling young barristers, hence the reworking of the Plan's distinctive initials to 'Lawyers' Assistance'.

The Needy Litigant Committee in my jurisdiction had a volunteer group to administer the plan, and a number of practitioners also volunteered to act *gratis* in civil matters, mostly domestic, landlord and tenant, that sort of thing, and the Court filing fees would be provided free of charge under the auspices of the Clerk of the Court.

The 'dock brief' would usually take place at the Criminal Arraignments before a Justice of the Supreme Court Trial Division, usually the Chief Justice, Campbell McLaurin or his successor James Valentine Hogarth Milvain. Counsel would attend for the purpose of setting trial dates in the High Court after committal for trial; Counsel for the Attorney General, that is, the Crown Prosecutor, would run the list. Every so often, an Accused would present without counsel, probably facing a serious charge. The Presiding Judge would simply point to one of the defence counsel in attendance and advise him/her that he/she was to defend the prisoner at trial. (The trial was usually the next afternoon, the charge was probably homicide.) Counsel appointed by the Court, and that was a great honour, would meet with the client, take instructions, and be ready to defend the case when it was scheduled, without fee. This system worked very well.

Young lawyers 'cut their teeth' on legal aid appointments; further, one would not eat steak for breakfast, but the eviction wolf was kept at bay. As a means for financially embarrassed citizens to obtain competent legal advice and representation, and as a training ground for young lawyers, the Alberta Legal Aid Plan was successful, operating with volunteer committees and professional administrators. I served as the Benchers' representative for a year or so on the local Legal Aid committee, and got first hand experience dealing with financial and bureaucratic issues arising.

Of the forty-four years I was in active practice in our Courts defending the basest and meanest of the Realm, I did the first twenty full years in the Legal Aid trenches, a soul-destroying vocation.

My first Legal Aid case was a young lout who stole an automobile. I pleaded him guilty to the euphemistic 'joyriding' and got him a suspended sentence. I then escorted him to the back and admonished him to learn well from this lesson, to which he responded, in gratitude for my free services, "Fuck you, asshole!" As I said in *Milt Harradence, The Western Flair*, that was the last time I confused criminal law practice with social work. My final Legal Aid case required me to drive to Rocky Mountain House in a snowstorm to vigorously defend a charge of homicide arising out of a drunken affray at a house party. The case cratered and the accused was discharged. My client was underwhelmed by my sterling forensic triumph; the proceedings must have been as intelligible to him as his memory of the house party. I was expecting at the least a weeping embrace, all his relatives throwing their ragged cloth caps into the air in "Huzzah!" Instead he feebly shrugged, turned, and walked away to freedom without looking back. I drove home through the snowstorm, averaging twenty miles per hour in velocity and $1.20 per hour in fees. It was exactly twenty years to the day that I had been Called to the Bar. I telephoned the Executive Director of the Legal Aid Society the next morning, said it was a slice, and had my name removed from the Legal Aid list. I had done my time.

Oh no, not Pro Bono! As for pro bono legal services, the current darling of the Law Society legacy initiative, I have a somewhat jaundiced view of these sorts of highly principled undertakings. I have to recognize that pro bono is one of the revolutionary upheavals in the legal profession in Canada this past half-century. That said, I have always found the inexplicable penchant of my fellow lawyers for do-gooding to be depressing. Doubtless many of them put on the selfless volunteer mask for their own self-aggrandizement or to increase their puissance. Some of them, I suppose, get themselves genuinely but inextricably involved in this or that uplifting project so that they can be suffused with the glory that shines around, *a la* Charles Darney, speaking of misdirected Revolutionary zeal: "It is a far, far better thing I do now, than I have ever done."

Not me. This new and revolutionary sacred cow project that took the profession by the throat starting in the late 1990s was the perfervid campaign for busy lawyers to donate their professional services to indigent litigants or perhaps certifiable lunatics for nothing. This was the pro bono sacred cow, and to speak against it was to invite opprobrium. One of the first shakedowns to take on complicated cases for no fee I got from one of my revered Seniors, a fellow Fellow of the American College of Trial Lawyers. The American College, having inducted to its ranks the cream of successful trial lawyers, instituted a subcommittee entitled "Access to justice and legal services" which took it upon itself to perpetrate the pro bono metaphysic to the Fellows. In December 1998, I received a letter from a senior partner of a very eminent legal firm, inviting me to volunteer for this 'challenging opportunity' to undertake 'high impact' cases, *gratis*, for indigent litigants. I responded at once, as I did not wish to volunteer or be volunteered to act in the capacity of pro bono/ legal aid nanny. I articulated my reasons for my declining any such honour thusly: 1. I did not want to do it. 2. Any barrister who had accepted as many Legal Aid briefs as I did in the first twenty years of my practice was as repelled by volunteerism as Arthur Koestler was by Communism. With tongue firmly in cheek, I opined that all Alberta Fellows would wish to defer to the appointment of (and here I named a prominent senior civil litigator) whom I was confident all would agree was the senior attorney most qualified for this 'challenging opportunity'. I noted that at this legal icon's sonorously omnipotent firm, "the partners speak of little else than pro bono, not to mention 'high-impact', cases." I concluded that I could not think of any Fellow better qualified to offer guidance to the legal team challenging by class action, say, Saskatchewan projected hoe-handle expansion for fiscal 1999, without pay.

I observed that, with respect, which is what lawyers say before they are going to insult somebody, the American College of Trial Lawyers need have no fear that aid to such worthy causes was wanting in Alberta. Example, the Canadian Bar Association (Alberta Branch and National) swarmed with perfervid volunteer social engineers who could handily be located at any number of stultifying cocktail parties. Why the Captains of this Profession should add to the current glut was beyond me.

One of the challenges confronting every newly minted incoming President of the Law Society of Alberta is taking the posture and striking a pose – as Balzac's absurd Captain Crevel, who "radiated self-satisfaction. He wore the aureole of complacency achieved by wealthy, self-made, retired shopkeepers" – now some sort of tradition, to define and adopt some worthy cause that will be the hallmark of her or his incumbency. Thus every year, in the Benchers' Hind-Quarterly featuring the opening words of wisdom from the recently installed poobah, one endures the author's ritual designation of his/her adopted new broom. Some of these were plain silly, others a predictable mishmash of previous high-sounding lofty goals, e.g., more hands-on with the Junior Bar, more "meaningful communication" to the public, more rigorous self-governance, that sort of bilge. Predictably, the current and fashionable pro bono varmint had to infect some new president, and in 2007 the President-Elect caught the bug rather badly. Indeed, he publicly declared to the Profession and the world at large that the embracing of pro bono ideals by the members of the Profession was the number one priority for his presidential year. Catch this excerpt from the President's Message of September 12, 2007:

> For the justice system to work, Albertans must have access to legal institutions and to legal advisers. We're proud of the services provided by Alberta lawyers, and we know they help people navigate their way through the legal system. We also know that Albertans with limited means can't always afford legal services. Alberta's lawyers provide thousands of hours of unpaid legal advice. Some of that is through volunteer work on boards or committees in a wide variety of non-profit organizations; much of it is provided quietly to clients who simply can't pay. This work is performed by lawyers for the greater public good -- pro bono -- so that people have access to the justice system. In our centennial year we have instituted a program to help even more Albertans of limited means. Pro Bono Law Alberta is a new non-profit organization that will promote access to justice in Alberta. It will create new opportunities for lawyers to provide pro bono (free) legal services to persons of limited means.

Poor old Kurtz had no concept of The Horror! One can only imagine the joy pervading the poverty-stricken public by loosing upon them volunteer capital markets and IPO specialists from the big international legal mills, to save them with free legal advice on how to paper the sale of a warship to the Central African Republic.

My learned friend the new President obviously worked round the clock, because two weeks after his uplifting public pro-bono announcement, he wrote me a letter. As part of its centennial pishposh, in May, 2007 the Law Society of Alberta had invited all the past and present Benchers it could track down to a fish fry and a falling on each other's necks at the Lougheed House. On receipt of the invitation, I had written the President to advise him that I would sooner attend a morticians' convention. I then received this letter:

> Dear Mr. Evans: Re: Commemorative Photo of Past and Present Benchers. On behalf of the Law Society of Alberta, I am pleased to present you with a commemorative photo of the Past and Present Benchers taken at our hundredth anniversary Bencher celebration in Calgary May 26. We are sorry that you were not able to attend. We hope that you will frame and hang this photo, and feel proud of your invaluable contribution to the Law Society of Alberta. Earlier this year, the Law Society of Alberta launched Pro Bono law Alberta, our legacy project directed at fostering and supporting the delivery of pro bono legal services to Albertans in need. Working in conjunction with all of the pro bono services providers in Alberta, PBLA is putting in place a number of exciting new pro bono initiatives and opening additional and easy ways for Alberta lawyers to provide pro bono legal services. One of the options for participating in Alberta's vibrant pro bono culture is through financial assistance, and PBLA is currently awaiting confirmation of its charitable status. We are hopeful that in lieu of payment for the photo you will consider a non-tax receiptable donation to PBLA in a suggested amount of $100.
>
> We hope that you will be able to join us in some of our centennial celebrations, and that you will enjoy this photograph over the years. Yours truly.

I wrote back to the Lord High Poobah of The Law Society:

"Re: Benchers' Mug Shots, Pro Bono Law, Other Importunations. I can't tell you how delighted I was to receive your letter together with an unabashed shakedown for a hundred dollars in overvalued Canadian currency, these escorting a 'commemorative photo' of three to four decades of old fogeys, now replaced by a gaggle of young fogeys. The last time I saw a collection of heads like those of the dignitaries immortalized in the photograph, it was in The Mummy's Tomb. Notwithstanding your hope 'that I will frame and hang this photo', I am more inclined to frame – by perjurious testimony, if necessary – and hang a number of the incumbents.

I advised the President that I fully appreciated that the advocates of pro bono were actuated by the most unselfish motives to provide Albertans of limited means with free professional legal services. I appreciated moreover that it was to be distinguished from the Alberta Legal Aid Plan, which paid some modest fees. Pro bono counsel volunteered their professional services *gratis*, which might be a sound reason why they should have their heads examined. The causes are practically all on the civil side, including the quagmires of poisonous domestic spasms and opaque administrative tribunals. I stated that we may anticipate that some prospective pro bono 'clients' in this brave new age will come from the ranks of those professional pests recently disenfranchised of clogging the courts by the Feds sensibly cutting off their taxpayer funding. Further, and sadly, I said, the experience of life and the law informs us that all too often the indigent client who wishes to become immersed in hideously protracted litigation of complexity and difficulty without paying fees is usually a bounder promoting a bogus claim. That, or he or she may be demonstrably insane. In either case, I opined that chances are good that this category of 'victimized citizen', in addition, is a sniveler and whiner, and an ingrate, and at the conclusion of a nasty and brutish episode reports his or her selfless volunteer unpaid counsel to the Law Society for some imagined transgression.

I concluded my diatribe:

> So, Mr. President, although I wish you and your associates
> well with Pro Bono Law Alberta, I'm more inclined to think
> that my hundred dollars would find a better home with the
> Salvation Army, and accordingly, have sent them a cheque in
> that amount this date. I am returning the photograph you so
> kindly sent me, as it would not be appropriate in the circum-
> stances for me to keep it."

The President, no doubt agitated by this missive, an attack upon
Alberta's 'vibrant pro bono culture', nevertheless was gracious
enough to write back to me and send me back the photograph. An
inspiring lot, alas, the Massed Pipes and Drums of the Past and Present Benchers.

3

LAW SOCIETY GOVERNANCE

The Benchers of the Law Society, that is, the Governors of the Profession in the Province elected by the Members, are a practical barometer for reading of the dramatic demographic changes that occurred in my profession starting in the 70s and surging into the 80s and 90s. There are now as many or more female Benchers than male Benchers; the average age is under forty; many are sole practitioners, family lawyers, criminal lawyers. At large in the profession, one witnessed the mushrooming of the big firms into national and then international law corporations with multiple partners and offices all over the world. This in turn gave rise to the litigation boutique and the specialty boutiques: virtually all of the disciplines of the law practice became specialist areas. Examples: family law, criminal law, probate, civil litigation, aboriginal law, many other areas. Within the practice of criminal law, one could specialize in commercial fraud, drug defences, homicide, driving offenses, that is, specialties and subspecialties. One positive result has been the essential split of the profession once more into barristers and solicitors: counsel work and document plodding each require specialty practitioners.

At the age of thirty-seven, I ran for the Office of Bencher of the Law Society of Alberta. This was literally unheard of at the time. The average age of the Benchers was fifty-five to sixty, their mean IQ was around sixty-seven, they were all male, they were all from Big Firms. As I have intimated in this history, they were anchored in hereditary privilege and oil or cattle money. The voting system was so rigged that, in accordance with the unspoken agreement of the big firms, all of the partners and legal associates of big firm A were required to vote for the Bencher candidates from the other big firms, and not to vote for any 'second class' or 'basely born' lawyer who was a sole practitioner or the very lowest of the low, a criminal lawyer. Inexplicably, I was elected. I had just attained my thirty-eighth birthday when I took office.

Two years later, the first female Bencher, my classmate Wallis Kempo QC, was elected, and in the next election, the redoubtable barrister Phyllis Smith QC who in time became the first female President of the Law Society of Alberta, and later the President of the Federation of Law Societies of Canada.

Up to about the 1980s, the governing council of the Law Society of Alberta, the Benchers, was dominated by a late-middle-age-to-elderly white male senior lawyer of the private club species. The early-day atmosphere of the Benchers' solemn convocations was indeed that of a private club. The old boys strove in good faith to address the urgent issues of self governance – among them education, discipline, ethics, touting, advertising – treating themselves to golf and dinner at the yearly Jasper retreat. But over time the members at large, demographically expanding, grew restive for more than representation by the remote.

Through the 1960s and 1970s the Benchers appeared largely nominated and elected by a combine, perhaps a cabal, of big firms. The voting protocol I have described lent itself to understandings. This was a fascinating study of Darwinian selection without Intelligent Design. As I have observed elsewhere, one would fail now to evidence this alleged practice with credible and admissible evidence, but like the mystery of Secret Handshakes, it was the practice.

By the mid to late 1980s, the Bar's demographics had altered dramatically, and the old selection process was permanently jarred. Membership increased exponentially with the Province's growth, the mean age lowered, more women every year entered the Profession and were elected to the Benchers, criminal lawyers and Crown prosecutors ran for the Bencher office and were elected. The result: younger incumbents representing a broader spectrum of membership interest. The old guard walked the egalitarian plank.

Major innovations in the Law Society occurred: a professional administration and bureaucracy; full time Law Society Legal Counsel and accountants; the endless Law Society self-reporting forms, the soporific accounting strictures, the absurd annual requirement to file some sort of a game plan for your 'personal development as a professional and improving your relationship with your clients' in the coming year.

My first year back in practice in 2012 – after my seven year writing interregnum – I simply wrote to the perfervid functionary overseeing this complete waste of time, "My object in the coming years is to improve myself as little as possible and to do nothing of redeeming social value." For 2013, I was similarly circumspect: "I'm seventy-four years old and I'm lucky just to be walking around. That's about as big a plan as I have."

The Law Society hired retired flatfeet as Law Society investigators of professional complaints; proletarian-friendly 'mission statements' emanated from the depths of the Law Society, all about Service to the Public; there was something mysterious called 'equity ombudspersons'. And, as a further nod to public participation in its solemn deliberations, the appointment of 'Lay Benchers'.

The Law Society now has a vast army of well-paid counsellors, uplifters, motivators, snoops and levellers employed by a vast bureaucracy (at the members' expense) to mentor and nurture inexperienced or incompetent lawyers and prosecute professional malefactors.

History is instructive. There is quite a remarkable parallel between the Imperialist Pretensions of the governors of the Members of the Law Society of Alberta and that of the Roman Republic circa 150 BC.

The Senate of Rome presided and debated in the Forum overlooking, and above, the circular amphitheater where the plebeian 'tribes' would gather to hear Senatorial decrees and, usually obediently, pass them into laws. Seated on benches right outside the Senatorial chamber were the Tribunes, elected representatives of 'the people', that is, the lower orders. The Tribunes, relatively powerful but not accorded Senatorial status, were entitled to listen to the Senatorial debates but not to participate in them, and were to place the Senatorial decrees (Advice) before the plebes (Consent).

The Senate was largely composed of patricians, that is, rich hereditary landowners and military leaders of powerfully connected families and dominant social hierarchies. Admitted to the Senatorial ranks were, on occasion, rich/powerful plebeians, but they were a minority and subjected to patrician snobbery. The introduction of Lay Benchers to the ranks of the elected Magistrates of the Law Society is essentially an analogous if reluctant acceptance of a couple of the more successful non-professional plebes to their ranks. These persons are appointed by the government of the day according to their political, business and social attainments and attachments; they essentially are Members of the Club who are expected to hew the majority line and not rock the establishment boat. As well, the current Deans of the two Law Schools are usually accorded Honorary Bencherdom, sans teeth.

The seating arrangement at the Law Society "Convocation" (you and I 'meet'; Benchers, like the Senate, 'convocate') is strikingly similar to the Senate-Tribune seating arrangement. The Benchers arrange themselves around their large circular inner table in the first-class seats; behind the privileged seats are ruder, second class seating accommodations for, e.g., the President or Vice-President for the time being of the Canadian Bar Association (Alberta Branch), the poobah of the Legal Education Society of Alberta, the Legal Archives Society of Alberta rep, and other lesser functionaries of their ilk. Each of them – as the Tribunes – not entitled to vote, but accorded adjacent seating just outside the forum and the privilege of listening to the debates, and required to be present to 'report' to the Benchers the estate and wishes of their tribe and to transmit the Benchers' decrees to their proletarian constituents.

This oligarchy has perpetuated itself. As I noted in my *Harradence* book, there is always room for one of the Gracchi brothers, Tiberius or Giauss, to foment an anti-establishment revolution. This revolution would have come about in that jurisdiction if one were aggravated by the formality of 'Recognizing the Benchers.'

Retained by the Attorney General of Alberta, I argued *Krieger v. Law Society of Alberta* in the Supreme Court of Canada in the spring of 2004. It had been nine years in litigation, issue being whether the Law Society or the Attorney General had jurisdiction respecting alleged bad conduct or bad faith on the part of a Crown prosecutor employed in Alberta. I won three zip in the Court of Appeal of Alberta, lost nine zip in the Supreme Court of Canada, the charge there led by my longtime mentor and friend The Hon. John C. Major, Puisne Justice of the Supreme Court of Canada.

Once in a while, a bright light emerges in law member governance: for example, Lindsay MacDonald QC, who was Law Society senior counsel for some years after being Court of Appeal counsel for the Department of the Attorney General, argued the matter through all courts for the Law Society. Although it was Lindsay Macdonald's appeal – as counsel for the Law Society who had lost at the appellate level – the Chief Justice indicated that they wanted to hear from me first, which was not a very good sign, and things went down from there. Bottom line is that the unanimous decision of the Court was delivered from the Bench allowing the Law Society's appeal, written reasons to follow, which indeed were fashioned by my mentor The Hon. Justice John Major and the Hon. Justice Frank Iacobucci, also a first class legal mind.

This to some extent added to the injury of nine-zip, because John C. Major QC when in practice had always had a very healthy view of the Benchers and their pomposities. He frequently appeared as counsel for Members facing conduct review hearings, usually disciplinary in nature. He would appear somewhat sceptically before the hearing panel. I particularly remember the occasion when he appeared before the full Benchers, eighteen strong, presiding in a major discipline matter. There was a litany to be slavishly followed by the Chairman of the Discipline Panel, in this case William Code

QC, a personage of some irascible temperament, and among the use-less questions counsel for the accused member was asked was "Do you recognize the Benchers?" The object, of course, was to establish that the member attorned to the jurisdiction of the panel. This being put imperiously to Jack Major QC by Code QC, Major QC replied, "Well I recognize some of you, but some of you I haven't met." Code got red in the face and put the question again. Major QC replied, "If you mean do you have jurisdiction to hear this matter? Yes, let's get on with it."

• • •

"Englishmen [who] tend to perish from the levels of remorse attending any offense graver than a leer."

— *Thomas Pynchon, Mason and Dixon*

I am repeating here a personal and humorous run-in I had with the Law Society's Made-in-Alberta Code of Professional Conduct.

As our Society lurched into the 1990s, approaching the comple-tion of its first century, our Governors were stirred by both hubris and ambition to manufacture the Alberta Law Society's very own Code of Professional Conduct. For decades, the Profession in Canada had managed very well under the tenets, strictures and prohibitions of the Code of Conduct promulgated by the Canadian Bar Associa-tion. Considering that this latter establishment is mainly noted for its cocktail parties (as a wag has said, "Going to a Canadian Bar func-tion is like going nowhere and talking to nobody about nothing") it had to be no minor accomplishment that its Wisers of an earlier day somehow managed to produce a codified ethical rule book. And any-way, it was more than sufficient, and most law profession governing bodies in other provinces simply adopted its precepts. These were then vigorously enforced, lawyers enjoying prosecuting lawyers.

Notwithstanding that, those who grow opulent then become ambitious, and seek to increase their puissance, and there was noth-ing for it but for the New Improved Benchers to promulgate an

Alberta code of professional conduct for lawyers, sweep out the old, duplicate much of it, and bring in a new look. For an example of the latter, rules of Crown prosecutorial conduct, which I have always maintained was none of the Law Society's business. I'm happy to state that, after nine years of litigation, I disagree with the unanimous decision of the Supreme Court of Canada that it is.

Among the jumble of new provisions designed to temper the worst excesses and secret vices of its members, the Law Society sprinkled capricious draconian measures. The most prominent among these was, of course, the strict prohibition against some felony called 'sexual harassment'. This was the darling of the feminist social engineers in the New Era, a high crime they thought appropriately punishable by death, following a kangaroo court trial with a reverse onus upon the accused. Among the more obvious definitions of what constituted sexual harassment lurked the absurd prohibition against 'leering'. (If that lot had spelled it "Learing" they could at least have accomplished a major social innovation by banning sorrowful family fallout and grief).

In addition to the offences proscribed in the bowl of prohibitions, it was possible to commit any offence identified by the Code's perfervid authors simply by attempting to commit it. An attempt, proved to the requisite Law Society culpability standard ("Where there's smoke there's smoke"), was a completed offence.

Moreover, the Code imposed a positive duty and obligation upon Members to report themselves to the Law Society should they transgress in any of the enumerated crimes and misdemeanors.

Accordingly, I was obliged to write to the Executive Director as follows:

> Sir. In accordance with the strictures of the Code of Professional Conduct of the Law Society, I hereby report myself to the Conduct Review processes for attempted leering, which delict I committed in observing an adult female person engaged in lengths in or about the swimming pool as I was departing the YMCA yesterday.

In the result, I was not formally charged, although the reactions of the Benchers were mixed. There was a small minority, I understand, who actually found my letter amusing. The more sober heads were shaken disapprovingly, down-turned mouths extant overall.

Speaking of professional conduct review and down-turned mouths brings to mind the 'non-reprimand reprimand', an intimidation device utilized by some pompous chairpersons of discipline panels where the panel, at the conclusion of the hearing, has dismissed the complaint and acquitted the member. That should be the end of it, but on occasion the chairperson, perhaps in view of the circumstances of the alleged delict, felt obliged to address the member in terms analogous to those employed by some High Court Judges on reluctantly acquitting a scum bag, the evidence falling short: "I find you not guilty. You keep this up, Smith, you'll be a dirty old man!" The non-reprimand reprimand might well be appropriate for criminal courts, but was certainly not a permissible expedient of the Benchers. On one such occasion, Bill Stillwell defending the member and the member acquitted, when the chairperson commenced "We remain concerned about the conduct of the member"...", Stillwell stood up and said "You just found him not guilty. That's it. We're leaving." They left.

We cannot scrutinize Law Society governance without commenting upon honorifics of the Profession reputedly awarded for excellence.

The Alberta Queen's Counsel appointment is conspicuous recognition every two years of practicing members of the Law Society who are considered senior counsel by the Government of the Province through the Office of the Attorney General. As I have noted elsewhere in this book, some aspirants to the Appointment as 'Her Majesty's Counsel learned in the law' actually appoint campaign committees and inundate the Chief Law Officer of the Crown or her/his Deputy with glowing letters from friends, colleagues, business associates, relatives, and clients.

The Distinguished Service Award is jointly sponsored by the Law Society of Alberta and the Canadian Bar Association (Alberta).

There are a considerable number of exemplary honorees appropriately recognized by the award, of course. I have observed over the years that many other distinguished colleagues have accomplished significant honours for the legal and public weal and have rendered very real service to the Profession and to the public but get passed over for the recognition.

With some honourable exceptions, some Benchers may be 'recognized' as public-spirited lawyers who are seeking a Queens Counsel appointment (it goes with the elected Office) and wanting to pad out their CVs for a federal Judicial appointment to a High Court, meanwhile being palsy with judges.

The saga of *Black v. The Law Society of Alberta* is an appropriate dénouement to this chapter. I touched briefly on it in the *Harradence* book.

> 'We are like Physicians, there is always enough Work for us,
> as we treat the Moral Diseases,' replies the Attorney, 'nor are
> we any more disposed than our Brother Doctors to meeting
> other folks' prices, hence our zeal in defending Monopoly.'
> — Thomas Pynchon, *Mason and Dixon*

A revolutionary disruption of the staid legal profession in Canada was heralded by the advent of national/international law firms. This marketing innovation was startling to the Alberta Benchers, who were always a few centuries behind.

I had been handily elected to the Benchers of the Law Society of Alberta for three consecutive terms commencing January, 1978. I had had quite enough of being a young fogey inserted into a nest of old fogeys by the end of my third term, said it had been a slice, and bowed out of the governance of my fellow lawyers. Four years went by quite fast, during which time it became clearer and clearer to me that the governors of the Law Society were far more concerned with the public image of lawyers in Alberta than they were for backing up individual members of the Bar who occasionally got into a contretemps with the said public. It had always been my experience that the great unwashed demanded far more of lawyers than they should be reasonably expected to give. I thought, however foolishly, that I might provide some sort of voice for the poor individual practitioners working out of a strip mall or defending the basest and meanest of the realm, working out of a telephone booth, so I ran again – topping the polls, inexplicably, which should tell the reader a thing or two about the public memory – and found myself back on the Law Society's governing body, negatively hailed as the 'born-again Bencher'. This was a pipe dream, of course, and after two more years of achieving nothing, this time I left the Benchers and stayed gone. The sequence I am about to relate took place, as best I recall, in the last year of my third consecutive term. The reason it is rather vivid is that it was during the auspicious occasion of the Benchers removing themselves to Red Deer for their Convocation that the action took place. At that time, I still had my ponytail and a full beard, and tended to dress less like a successful lawyer, which in Alberta meant looking like an Italian pimp, and more like the scrofulous fellow that deep down I was. One important item on the Red Deer agenda was the application of a very senior and respected Alberta practitioner, Robert Black QC, to the full Benchers asking them to reconsider their absurd rule that prohibited national law firms to associate with Alberta Law firms. I observed in the *Harradence* book, in a conspicuous footnote:

> The Benchers proposed and passed the rule on the specious pretext that they could not oversee disciplinary matters of national firms, but the real reason was crass Alberta protectionism for fear of the greater talent elsewhere which would rabbit off their major clients.

I have some recollection of the debates that had preceded the almost unanimous passing of the rule: one other independent minded Bencher named Hugh Landerkin and I were the only two who voted against it. The debate, if one could call it that, was highlighted by sonorous gusts of wind from Benchers who, coincidentally, were senior partners in large Alberta firms, and who thought they might feel a bit of a client departure chill from a local firm being associated with some heavy hitters in Toronto or Montreal.

Of course, the points they made were not couched in exactly those terms. They were couched in highflying rhetoric bemoaning the absence of necessary checks and balances in invigilating conduct review of partners in Alberta firms domiciled in 'foreign jurisdictions' like remote Ontario and Quebec. Never mind the advent and efficacy of computers. Or, for that matter, the requirement that those partners also become members of the Alberta Bar. It happened that the appearance of Mr. Black QC and his learned counsel, a former president of the Law Society, Jim Beames QC, was scheduled for the morning following my own unscheduled sojourn back in Calgary. The more auspicious event occurring in Calgary was a concert at the Jubilee Auditorium featuring the great Stan Rogers and his excellent folk group, with the opening act my great and good pals The Wild Colonial Boys.

My old mates John Martland and Mansel Davies, the two most important legs of our former three-legged stool band The Old Triangle, were principals of the Wild Colonials. As soon as the Benchers rose for the day from their solemn and soporific deliberations, I jumped in the Jeep and hightailed it back to Calgary. The concert was a rousing success, and the two bands together with a phalanx of their supporters adjourned to the salubrious precincts of the Unicorn Pub, where we all proceeded to get shit-faced. There was a great deal of ale quaffing and sea shanty singing and the greatest good fellowship. I staggered home by the back alleys at about 4 a.m., feeling no pain. I experienced a great deal of pain early the next morning – my cerebellum was fragile, and my mouth tasted like a bird had shat in it.

Through the fog, I realized that I had to get back to Red Deer for the crucial application and debate. Somehow I managed to throw on some old jeans and a faded sweatshirt that might have been emblazoned with an outrageous slogan and a pair of old sneakers. I hauled myself into the Jeep and aimed it for the central snowbelt city.

By the time I got to Red Deer, got parked, and got myself into the meeting – pardon me, convocation – room, I was unfashionably late, and the application had already commenced. The only open chair at the Benchers' horseshoe table was one right beside the formidable Alan Hunter QC, who from day one had taken a very aggressive opposition to national firms marrying up with Alberta firms. I must have looked, particularly to the applicant and the senior solicitors from his firm who accompanied him, a most unprepossessing specimen. I saw Mr. Black whispering to his learned counsel, who replied, indicating me, as I became aware of the eyes of his associates goggling at me, wondering "Who the hell is that scrofulous hippie!" The Benchers took turns peppering the distinguished applicant and his learned counsel with questions. I vividly remember Alan Hunter confronting the very senior Mr. Black QC with, "And how do we know that the partners in your firm not resident in Alberta will conduct themselves ethically, Mr. Black?" To which Mr. Black spiritedly responded, in no uncertain terms, "You have my word, Mr. Hunter." There was an uneasy silence

At that point, I took the opportunity to raise my hand and was recognized by the Chair. "Mr. Chairman," I said,

> "I have studied this matter at great length. I am fully satisfied that permitting national firms to associate with Alberta firms is the most desirable concept, particularly in these days of burgeoning globalism, and national firms can surely only benefit the profession in this province with their more sophisticated and worldly perspective."

Or something to that effect. The looks of utter astonishment on the faces of Mr. Black QC and his associates remain memorable. The Benchers, naturally, indicated they would take time to consider the matter, thanked the applicant and his counsel and his associates, and adjourned the matter. Of course, they turned the applicant down, and thus the matter was litigated in the courts. The Benchers chose to litigate this to the Supreme Court of Canada at a considerable cost to its members, and lost, plus costs against the Law Society. To the best of my knowledge, I understood that the recovered costs, or a goodly portion of them, were magnanimously donated by Mr. Black QC to a worthy charity. I learned then as I know now, the solemn deliberations of the Benchers of the Law Society of Alberta could always benefit from a little healthy criticism. Every so often, they and their ilk, High Court judges, e.g., need to be reminded that they put on their pants one leg at a time just like plain folks.

4

THE CHARTER OF RIGHTS

"Everyone has rights. No-one has responsibilities."

— Hon. J. V. H. Milvain, retired Chief Justice

There has been a great deal of discussion, and continues to be *ad infinitum*, respecting the care and feeding of the *Canadian Charter of Rights and Freedoms*, proclaimed in 1982. I say at the outset that I really do not have anything substantial to add to the discussion. *The Globe and Mail* edition of Saturday, December 30, 1989 included a well-researched piece by Kirk Makin headlined 'Charter cases rise over legal landscape'. He notes: "Canadians fell in love with the concept of rights."

The writer surveys the most significant Supreme Court of Canada decisions during the 80s, the lynch pin being the 1981 constitutional patriation decision holding that the federal government, with the agreement of a substantial number of provinces, could legally patriate and amend the Constitution. In a 1985 Alberta case, the Court "signaled that the Charter would not be stifled at birth," that the approach to the Charter was to be 'liberal and expansive." In 1986, the Court held unconstitutional laws may be struck down if the government cannot show they are "demonstrably justified in a free and democratic society." In 1989, the Court indicated it would take a liberal view of discrimination.

Begin at the Charter with the end: Section 52(1): "The Constitution of Canada is the supreme law of Canada, and any law that is inconsistent with the provisions of the Constitution is, to the extent of the inconsistency, of no force or effect." Subsection 2 states: "The Constitution of Canada includes (a) the Canada Act 1982, including this Act;"

The Charter makes pretty good reading. It purports to declare and enshrine and preserve every right and freedom of every nature and kind in an organic document that is the supreme law of the land: fundamental freedoms, e.g., religion, thought, Press, peaceful assembly, association; citizen mobility; 'life, liberty and security of the person'; security against unreasonable search or seizure; no arbitrary detention; rights on arrest; no subjection to cruel and unusual punishment. The list is long.

The 'notwithstanding clause' frequently referred to is S. 33 (1) of the Charter: "Parliament or the legislature of a province may expressly declare in an act of Parliament or of the legislature, as the case may be, that the Act or a provision thereof shall operate notwithstanding a provision included in section 2 or sections 7 to 15 of this Charter."

The 'deal of discussion' includes the allegation that some Courts of this country have encroached upon the prerogatives of the federal and provincial legislatures under the authority of the Charter. *Ultra vires* decisions founded in the Charter may be legislatively invalidated by invoking the 'notwithstanding clause', but few elected bodies want to take that rather drastic step. A notable exception was the matter of commercial bilingualism in Quebec. The writer of the 1989 *Globe* article points out that when the Court declared Quebec French-only signs legislation unconstitutional the then Premier invoked the 'notwithstanding clause' to accomplish the legislative intent.

So much has been written and prognosticated about 'the Charter' by myriads of judges and gaggles of academics and legal bloggers that one hesitates even to broach the subject, save in the most general terms of recognizing its stranglehold upon the law of the land as the supreme constitutional authority. The hills swarm with professionally recognized experts on the Charter and constitutional law. The perceptive and knowledgeable writer Rex Murphy, *National Post,* Saturday, May 31, 2014, is critical of the suggestion that the Charter is an "automatic authenticator of 'progressive' values'" simply because one can securely parrot "It's in the Charter" as with Biblical corroboration. He argues that the Charter "is always open to interpretation and amendment."

Some Charter interpreters cite the 'notwithstanding clause' and vent related angst that some Courts purport to impose their priorities and set government policy on the authority of the Charter, rather than adhering to their long-standing role to interpret and enforce duly enacted laws. One author, Bob Runciman (*National Post* July 15, 2014) notes this, and argues that "While the Charter increases the scope of judicial power, that basic principle remains intact."

There is also the very readable book *The Charter Revolution and the Court Party*, by University of Calgary Professor Ted Morton, of the nationally recognized Calgary School of conservative political thought. His book argues that the Charter gave the Supreme Court of Canada considerable power to alter government policy. He refers to a whole host of rulings in recent decades. Examples: striking down of abortion laws, voting rights for convicts, restricted extradition for criminals facing capital punishment abroad, all of which attracted conservative criticism. Opposition to Charter-inspired judicial activism is found in nests of conservatives all across Canada. Preston Manning, highly respected former Reform Party leader, noted that the Charter "in essence, undermined the supremacy of Parliament and gave the judges a much more active role in overriding decisions of Parliament." Opposition to this new judicial activism is the reason why Western premiers insisted on the notwithstanding clause to contain the Charter's power.

Traditionalists argue that Parliamentarians and legislators legislate – responsible government at work – and judges judge, their role to interpret the legislation. Critics say that Judges cannot just make up laws and ignore the legislative intention. The concern is that, overruling considered legislation by our elected representatives, judges can interpret the Charter as they wish and strike down legislation if they think it inadequate or unacceptable, that is, unconstitutional. It is alleged that a lot of judges are guided by their own individual biases, hence the swipe by the late Justice McClung inveighing against "Rights-active judges privateering in Charter waters."

The short-term solution that commends itself to the more extreme opponents of 'judicial activism' is to replace several of Her Majesty's Justices with sounder models that have not had their gears tinkered with by egalitarian legislation. The opponents are confident that Oliver Cromwell would endorse this necessary purging as a cruel necessity.

I have written earlier that in this *contretemps*, I held no brief for either party, but I did write my good friend Buzz McClung with the admonition of the great Oliver Wendell Holmes that agreed with his championship of the exclusive right of the elected representatives in the Legislature to make law, and the contrary opinion of the equally gifted H.L. Mencken that sometimes it was necessary for Courts to intervene to strike down, amend, or remedy legislation, because most politicians would vote even for cannibalism if it got them elected.

To curb social tinkering judges, it was anticipated that recourse might be had by the provinces and/or the federal government to invoke the notwithstanding clause and vacate court rulings in their jurisdiction. Regrettably, moan some critics, this has not been utilized enough.

My take on all this? Notwithstanding all the pros and cons of Charter-inspired litigation inviting bold judicial activism, my bottom line is to recognize the Charter revolution's profound effect on the practice – my practice – of criminal law defence.

Many of the rights and freedoms enumerated by the senior Trudeau's Charter goblins – the important ones (the 'Rights', not the goblins) – were part and parcel of the English common law probably since *Magna Carta*, and thus became the prevailing law of Canada and Australia and United Kingdom colonies. Canadians have always enjoyed fundamental freedoms: speech, religion, elections, independent judges, trial by jury. We did not need a written law to affirm them or declare them. The suggestion that these were 'new' rights and freedoms thought up by the Liberal government of the day is a bit much. As a criminal lawyer, I practiced my profession in exercise and enjoyment of these rights on behalf of my clients long before the Charter was enacted.

The question arises whether, during the forty years up to my going on the inactive list of the Law Society for the first time in March 2005, I ever made a Charter application in all of those years. The answer is: one application. A client of mine had been detained at a police check stop, submitted to the roadside alcohol check device, failed, allegedly declined the Breathalyzer, and was charged with refusing a breath test. Somewhere along the way, probably at Criminal Lawyer's Summer Camp, I heard one of my colleagues talk about a recent Saskatchewan study on the roadside alcohol check device. I decided to make a demand on the Crown for disclosure of the Saskatchewan studies. This I did, in writing, and served it upon the prosecuting attorney. I heard nothing back. I renewed my request, and got no response. In the result, I made a motion before a Provincial Court Judge in Calgary to stay the prosecution on the grounds of non-disclosure. I made my submission: I cannot remember what the prosecution argued. The presiding Provincial Judge had concerns, and in due course a written decision was rendered that judicially stayed the Information. Amazement! That was the only time, to my best recollection, that I ever invoked the Charter of Rights and Freedoms on behalf of a client.

Charter apps have of course been cranked up since then. Speaking to the concept of *ex post facto verboten*, there is nothing like mixing a little Latin with German in treating of 'investigative necessity' and 'probable cause'. The abolition of *ex post facto* reasoning has stood the criminal justice tradition on its head. Better, indeed, that rather than one innocent person being wrongfully convicted, ten guilty persons go free, and critics say that is more often the case since the inception of the *Charter of Rights and Freedoms*. I have previously called the *Charter of Rights* the barter of rights: persons accused of public crime in this country can sometimes trade a

Charter 'violation' for a lesser charge or a lighter penalty, or an early release. The dystopian mentality recalls Arthur Koestler in *Darkness at Noon*: "The means has become the end, and darkness has come over the land."

Criminal defence lawyers have to grasp nettles, and it helps to have tools. New generations of defence lawyers wield the *Charter* sometimes as a sharp-edged weapon, Saladin's scimitar or the samurai sword, other times as a bludgeon. Most prosecutors start with the proposition that the client is badly wanted in a federal penitentiary. That is, he has been caught red-handed, if one were to apply *ex post facto* reasoning: "Dead to rights, it's a fair cop, Guv!" Aha, but for the Barter of Rights! Instead of painting for the Court a picture of the client as the Angel Gabriel, today's criminal defence lawyer pursues a Charter remedy.

Example: Cops tap phones of 'persons of interest'; get information of a planned drop-off; swoop, seize, charge. At trial, the court is plunged into the throes of what is called the 'Garofoli Application', to strike down the phone intercept order and, ergo, the pinch. Was there alleged material nondisclosure of relevant facts to the Issuing Judge, which might have caused the Issuing Judge not to have issued the intercept order? That is, make him or her into a Non-Issuing Judge. A shot in the dark sometimes hits the target.

Wiretap has been roundly condemned in some quarters, characterized as being, apparently, somewhat unsporting. Some legal authorities have embraced the suggestion that electronic eavesdropping on suspected criminals endangers the law-abiding citizens of a liberal democracy. Contrasting cases in point: In the United States the Courts have consistently ruled that the originator of a text or an email maintains no privacy right once the message has been dispatched into the outer ether. Some Canadian courts have taken a more restrictive approach, several recent decisions finding that senders of texts and emails have a reasonable expectation of privacy in their outgoing communications.

Therefore, the most positive benefit of the Charter has been that it has returned the sporting element to criminal litigation.

It is hardly surprising that many law-abiding citizens who are non-lawyers, and who reel from the daily round of mayhem and mindless violence that gluts the news of the day and sells media advertising, decry and complain about some courts making the world safe for the less savory elements of society, and that in itself threatens the security of the citizen which is part and parcel of the social contract subscription.

Guaranteeing that criminal suspects receive equal justice from the community would conform with many fair-minded persons' approach, being as they are unlawful characters who are also entitled to the protection of the rule of law that is enforced by the elected representatives of the general population. What has happened with the pre-eminence of the *Charter of Rights* in criminal litigation in the mind of the average citizen is that the rule of law can be a weapon used by persons accused of crime against the rest of us. Hence the *Charter's* derisive nickname at the Criminal Bar: the Criminals' Code.

There were significant Alberta charter cases. As I have written elsewhere, the prosecution *Regina v. Keegstra* (1990) is prominent, as one would expect of the Charter case symbolic of the monumental, ancient, and archetypal struggle of Light versus Dark. 'Freedom of expression' was in issue. My view is that those who spout malevolent fictions should just be ignored, not made into international news stories. No publicity, no victory for the Darth Vaders of the universe.

A monumental Charter case, *Regina v. Stinchcombe*, emanated also from Alberta. *Stinchcombe* is probably the most significant revolutionary criminal law decision in Canada. Crown disclosure was confirmed as a principle of fundamental justice. I deal with disclosure in Chapter 6.

I made the following comments in the Law Society of Alberta 100th Anniversary book, *Just Works: Lawyers in Alberta 1907 - 2007*, and consider them worth repeating in this chapter: The Charter darkened the skies of criminal litigation with a locust swarm of paper, paper, paper. Reported criminal clients' Charter cases number two hundred to three hundred thousand bales that now overflow their warehouse storage at Hoboken, in the old Norddeutscher-Lloyd pier, replacing all the bad poetry written in North America since Smith and Pocahontas. Exaggerating ever so slightly, in the Law Society book I opined that in Canada there are something like 180,000 Charter applications every hour; two percent of them have merit.

Rigorous judicial deployment of the Charter has curbed the enthusiasm of a lot of good old-line cops, who were used to having dodgy confessions admitted in the Crown's case, and illegitimate seizures marked at trial as evidence against the accused. As a Crown prosecutor employed by the Attorney General for almost five years in the pre-charter era, 1968 to 1973, I got along well with the cops, municipal and federal, and we chalked up a pretty high rate of criminal convictions, as did my colleagues. The defence was often reduced to 'trial by ambush', or making a deal, ten years with parole being preferable to life without parole.

A certain respect for police officers investigating serious crime not having to wear kid gloves has always been there, and even as late as 2013 in a 4-3 ruling in a search and seizure case involving a veteran police officer and a sniffer dog, Mr. Justice Michael Moldaver of the Supreme Court of Canada, one of the top criminal defence lawyers in his day, wrote, as reported by the excellent legal journalist Sean Fine, "in typically blunt fashion that not every police move should be 'placed under a scanning electron-microscope'."

By the time the excesses of the late Conservative government came to the fore and excited public condemnation in or about 2015 – build more jails and throw away the key; mandatory minimum sentences so the judge was stripped of exercising judicial discretion in a particular case and was reduced to a rubber stamp; politically-loaded judicial appointments to the high courts; longer incarceration for persons found not criminally responsible – the Charter came much in play in criminal litigation, outstripping other conventional defences in gaining acquittals for some accused persons. I am not carping at this: many a person accused of public crime has quite properly been acquitted by Charter intervention. And there is always the saving argument for the Crown of section 24(1), that is, that even where there are proven Charter violations, the accused is not necessarily cut loose if in the Court doing so it would cause the administration of justice to fall into disrepute. Not every violation of the Charter necessarily results in Charter relief.

Mr. Justice Michael Moldaver was a prominent Leader of the Criminal Defence Bar before elevation to the Ontario Superior Court, the Ontario Court of Appeal, and then the Supreme Court of Canada. In 2012, then on the Ontario Court of Appeal, speaking at Osgoode Hall he gave a speech, as reported by the excellent legal journalist Sean Fine of the *Globe and Mail* newspaper, in which he complained about defence lawyers who "trivialize" the Charter of Rights and Freedoms with unnecessary rights claims. His comment that some defence lawyers mount frivolous Charter applications that can cause unnecessary case backlogs got a lot of flack from defence lawyers and some politicians. Justice Moldaver countered that he had "the highest regard" for competent lawyers and that they were the "backbone" of the justice system, but he asked counsel to be responsible in bringing Charter applications and to take a hard look before they did. He suggested that the court system was overburdened with long, complex cases, including needless, futile challenges under the Charter from some defence lawyers.

I also endorse enthusiastically the comments of Justice Moldaver, speaking to the deteriorating relations between the prosecution and the defence in the post-Charter era. He is quoted In *The Globe and Mail* newspaper in 2015 by Mr. Fine.

In sum, he was concerned that both Crown and defence lawyers had to be more responsible, and trust each other. He said the stakeholders in our justice system should work together and act responsibly in delivering quality justice. He noted that some trial judges worried about being overturned, and therefore tended to err on the side of caution. Defence counsel raised Charter motions about which they were dubious, to avoid facing an incompetent counsel allegation in an appellate court. Prosecutors were reluctant to make tough calls because they felt they did not get backing from their superiors.

The Justice noted that he had done a lot of murder trials, and most of them took seven or eight days. Homicide trials today might go seven or eight weeks or even seven or eight months.

· · ·

Rights and freedoms without corresponding responsibilities have signified a new era in the practice of law. Professor Ted Morton, quoted earlier, speaks of an "ideological homogeneity in Canadian law schools: 'To train for the legal profession is to study the politics of victimology'." Lovely line, that; there is virtue in victimhood. The inclusive and accommodating policies of our brave new legal world have added onerous challenges to the practice of law, particularly in the Courts.

As I have observed in an earlier writing, I regret that among these challenges are: the metamorphoses of the objective Crown Prosecutor, the 'Minister of Justice', to 'victims' advocate', and the objective defence counsel to 'conspiracy theorist'; trial sensationalism by the media; the proscription of advocacy; the abridgement of meaningful sanctions for mendacious witnesses; the conviction of accused persons on the uncorroborated testimony of unsworn witnesses, and upon the absurd opinions of junk science; the proliferation of social media and the forfeiture of privacy. All of these dubious developments incidental to the positive revolutionary changes within my profession have as their concomitants the erosion of the fair trial.

I conclude with the observation that the *Charter* has side effects, for example the currently fashionable lawsuit and intervenor facilitator called 'the Court Challenges Program'. This taxpayer-funded program was mercifully expunged by the Harper Tories – one of their more positive initiatives in 2006 – but as at February 2016 was predictably resurrected and reinstated by the new Liberal government in keeping with their professed 'diversification and inclusiveness' philosophy. The Court Challenges Program is a federal program that funds, with taxpayers money, constitutional lawsuits, presuming that governments are from time to time passing unconstitutional laws.

That is, the government can be sued by a clutch of citizens who think that a Canadian law violates the *Charter of Rights and Freedoms*. Constitutional litigation is lengthy and hideously expensive, and the taxpayers are left in the position of paying for the government to defend the case and paying the qualifying plaintiffs to bring the case.

A number of matters discussed in this chapter I have written elsewhere, and make no apology for repeating my observations here. The serious issues arising from the negative revolutionary developments over the past decades challenging our Profession will have to be addressed – and, I hope, redressed – by the Law schools and educational and ethical legal organizations, by the Benchers of the Law Societies of Canada, and by succeeding generations of practicing lawyers.

5

THE FEMALE ASCENDANCY

"What's to be said for an era. Well, the rise of women is the most successful revolution in recorded history, and many of us have been happy to live through it."

— Robert Fulford in the December 21, 2013 ed., *National Post*

The female ascendancy and the end of the old boy network was by far the most significant revolutionary transformation of my profession.

When I graduated from law school in 1963, the profession was dominated by old privileged white guys in large firms: they dominated the Bench, they dominated the Benchers, they dominated the ranks of senior counsel, and they fulfilled their manifest destiny by rigid application of the doctrine "old age and treachery will overcome youth and skill." They were anchored in hereditary privilege and oil or cattle money. There were four women in my law class of about sixty students. All the professors were male. When we graduated, there were only seven women practicing law in the province of Alberta. There were no women judges, no women Benchers, and one can reasonably be sure that there were no women directors of public companies.

Three women in my law class had exceptional careers, and each was instrumental in advancing the cause of women in the profession of law: Anne Russell ended her admirable career as a Senior Justice of the Court of Appeal of Alberta; Wallis Kempo QC was elected the first female Bencher of the Law Society of Alberta, and was appointed to the Tax Court of Canada; Alice Ostrowercha practiced successfully as a pioneer lawyer in the Northwest Territories before continuing practice in British Columbia, raising a family, and serving four consecutive terms as Mayor of North Saanich, B.C.

I reiterate here some of the material that I referred to in my article in the Law Society book *Just Works*. For the origins of the female ascendency in Alberta, the reader should read the leading and classic paper "Ladies in Law in the 1960s," by the Honourable Justice Anne H. Russell. In her Ladyship's speech to the 1998 Legal Archives Society of Alberta annual historical dinner, she noted

> The real turning point for women in the legal profession was in the 1960s…In 1960 there were no women on the Bench at any level, no female Benchers, no female directors of the Bar Association, and no female law professors. Only about seven were on the active practicing list….

Given that there was blatant discrimination and male bone-headedness in those early years following our graduation, she states, fairly and graciously, "… in my experience, the overwhelming majority of the men in the profession were decent, tolerant, and accommodating."

Although the 1960's ladies in law were too early to take the turning female tide at the flood, that "vital and productive feminist movement that flourished after us," Russell J.A. observes that her 1960s contemporaries made a significant contribution to the Profession "and the ease with which other women could later enter it."

Apropos of Justice Russell's balanced comments of discrimination countered with accommodation, throughout the early course of my practice I encountered considerable resistance among my male colleagues to women lawyers and judges. Many of my male colleagues were, and remained, irretrievably rooted and hopelessly mired in the late 19th early 20th centuries mindset. The suggestion of a woman on the Bench or a partner in a firm or a director of a public company or a Minister of the Crown was anathema to the old boy network. It has therefore been a long, hard struggle for women, one foot forward, two back, two feet forward. Rosemary Brown, Executive Director of Match International, an Ottawa-based NGO working with women in the third world and Canada, had some telling observations in the *Globe and Mail* edition of December 30, 1989, on the frustratingly slow but steady advance of women in the 80s. Positive advances included appointments of outstanding women to the Supreme Court of Canada, and the benefit of the number of women elected to public office at all levels of government and the increase in the ranks of women entering post-secondary institutions. She remained concerned that women's economic status had not at that time changed substantially. That is still an issue in our society.

She states: "For me, the past decade has been a roller-coaster ride of raised hopes, dashed dreams, tedious plodding, horror and brutality, as well as of surprising developments and incredible victories."

I distinctly recall, even in the late 80s, an article in a Toronto magazine about my prominent colleague at the criminal bar Michelle Fuerst, entitled "Not a job for a lady." The Hon. Michelle Fuerst is now a supervising Superior Court Judge in Ontario. Women are today among the top criminal lawyers in Canada. One of the finest counsel and best cross-examiners I ever encountered in my fifty years of practice was civil litigation specialist Eleanore Cronk, Fellow of the American College of Trial Lawyers, now a Justice of the Ontario Court of Appeal. In a recent letter to the *National Post* decrying the fact that there are so few women executives and on boards of corporate directors, a correspondent asks: "Why do men still dominate corporate culture in Canada? It is both a huge waste of talent and proof that gender bias is still alive and well." She goes on to observe that women are outperforming men in schools and universities and in the workforce.

Boris Johnson, the very personable former Mayor of London and post-Brexit UK Foreign Minister, wrote on 'female ascendancy', which he called "the biggest social revolution of our lifetime". He enthused: "Look at those girls go! – Women now make up 57% of university entrants, and they outnumber men in every subject including maths and engineering. This thing is huge, and it is happening at every level…"

The speed of the female juggernaut and the decline and fall of the male plutocracy was ineluctable. Today at least fifty percent of appointees to the Federal and Provincial Courts must be, and are, women. Over fifty percent of law graduates in Canada are women, and they dominate the awards and moots and earn the highest marks, eclipsing most of the male students struggling to keep up. The current Prime Minister of Canada has made it a telling point for his administration that at least fifty percent of his Cabinet at any time are highly qualified women.

A conspicuous leader of the female ascendancy in my Profession is the Honourable Catherine Fraser, the Chief Justice of Alberta. She is a brilliant legal analyst, an incredibly hard-working judge, possessed of a formidable and rigorous intellect, and a most able leader of the Judiciary, and I have always held her in the highest esteem.

My Profession, and the Western world, have changed, and for the good. Putting this revolution somewhat more graphically, I am repeating unapologetically what I wrote in *Just Works: Lawyers in Alberta, 1907 – 2007*, and quoting from my first Memoir *Milt Harradence: The Western Flair*, with some updates, because I consider it quite permissible to plagiarize oneself, and anyway, my observations do not stale with repetition.

> The strident…female lobby took over this Profession in the down and dirty manner of a longshoreman cleaning out a waterfront saloon. On an elementary level, this victory - and it was a clear victory - has been wholly admirable: the conspiratorial ambitions of many a male fascist bigot have gone down in flames as women appropriated their previously unassailable prerogatives and ascended en masse to their places in the Profession and on the

Courts. Indeed, the elevations of female persons to all levels of Courts have been epidemic. Some of them are truly exceptional jurists.... the Alberta Court of Appeal became known to the Criminal Bar (affectionately, natch) as 'The All Girls Band'.

My text continues:

The female phalanx threw off the yoke of old boy privilege with a ringing collective voice that shattered glass ceilings, as exuberant as the Ride of the Valkyrie, and as sobering as the worst excesses of the French Revolution. A meticulous statistical study of the rise of women in the Profession would glaze the eyeballs of Euclid, but it would be a character-building examination for all first-year male law students to have to commit its paragraphs to memory and publicly recite the entire study before advancement to second year, in the manner of schoolchildren's enforced recitation of Robespierre's 'The Objects and Principles of the Revolution'.

In closing this sincere tribute in my book to the marvelous ladies of my Profession, I cannot resist tacking on this Portrait of the Female Judge as a Young Woman, which I originally authored for the Law Society 100th Anniversary coffee table book (No, I am not being uncivil to my female colleagues, I am simply a commentator and observer with an irrepressible sense of humour.)

One wishes to highlight the sonorous splendor of the photographs of the Judiciary, produced at great public expense, that adorn all of the Court Houses of the province. There is no escaping their disapproving glares. The comments for the Law Society book that I mustered at that time relating to the photographs of the female Judges of the species were, understandably, suppressed, that tome not the appropriate place, perhaps, for levity, let alone ribaldry. I had tried to sneak it in, the chances being good that a few surreptitious lines would escape the vigilance of the censorship board. (The

Law Society book censorship board was, I believe, peopled by the same Comstocks who made up the new Code of Professional Conduct). No, my piece was cashiered. Chastened, I reserved the comments for a more appropriate venue, which happens to be this chapter.

> Empowered female lawyers invariably "dress for success" in what they call "power threads"; some consider that they "make a statement". Once appointed to the Bench, however, the Hon. Provincial Court Judgess (a perfectly good word: see 'giantess') or Madam Justice cannot choose the adroit combination of attire that heretofore has enhanced her aura. She is relegated to the costume of the Court, its uniform, short of imaginative innovation with the 'bands' of Office, female judges often eschewing the austere starched curate model for a lacy jabot or designer choker. Whatever. Otherwise, it is the baggy black vest with Squire Trelawney cuffs, and the red or blue trimmed polyester gown. If she is a "Red Judge", she is troubled to find that the shade of scarlet designated the Court does not match her lipstick. It is therefore understandable that the Court photographers' female subjects would seek subtle ameliorations to their physiognomies falling short of radical plastic surgery but sufficient to counter the sort of vile observation found in Evelyn Waugh's Diary: "She had a face like a pie!"
>
> Their results? Photoshop botox injections. Many of the photos of female Judges are masterpieces of the airbrush-meisters' art. I myself have been impressed by the notably glamorized versions of several of the subjects.
>
> Some of these results approach transfiguration, even metamorphosis. Such portraits have a cruel denouement. Perhaps male Learned Counsel is not personally acquainted with the Lady Judge before whom his trial is scheduled. Having worshipped a vision of loveliness in the portrait, he dons a fresh court shirt and clean starched tabs in breathless anticipation. He is expecting, perhaps, Ms. Christie Brinkley. "Order in the Court!" Enter Boaty McBoatface! AARRRGGGHHH!

6

DISCLOSURE

The ethical duty of full disclosure in civil cases was imported to the criminal process by the Supreme Court of Canada in *R v. Stinchcombe,* circa 1991: the fullest and most comprehensive disclosure must be made in a timely fashion by the Crown to the defence of all material and relevant facts and evidence in possession or control of the Crown or of the investigating police authority, whether for the Crown or for the defence, a breach of which is very serious ethical misconduct and a Charter violation which, if grave enough, can award an accused person a Court stay of proceedings.

The only illumination I can bring to this revolutionary development is my earlier encounter with the selfsame William Stinchcombe. It is not without great good humour that I recall this encounter. It was 1969 or 1970, I was with the Crown Prosecutors' office in Calgary. Every so often one of the seven of us had to man the pit and provide 'particulars' of a current charge before the Courts to defence counsel who requested them. So we would have a sheaf of files, usually consisting only of the police report and a copy of the Information, but sometimes holding witness statements and stuff of that sort. In those days, there was no such concept as 'Crown disclosure'. It was customary to informally give verbal 'particulars', that is, an outline of the case for the Crown, without providing witness names or witness statements to the defence, who were not considered entitled to that information, however helpful to the defence. Moreover, to be blunt, although one routinely gave particulars to most of the defence counsel who, in the days of a small Criminal Bar, were well known, it was a somewhat capricious and even arbitrary process, as one might not be inclined to give information to a defence counsel who might be out of favour.

There are at random points in history fortuitous confluences and encounters that illuminate subsequent events. The reader should not dismiss these seminal events as 'coincidences'.

One late afternoon a pleasant young fellow in a three-piece suit presented himself to my office, advising that he sought particulars in a case pending before the Court. I asked him his name, and he replied "Bill Stinchcombe." I asked him where he was working, and he said that he was articled to a prominent defence counsel currently making a name. Instead of giving any particulars whatsoever to this gentleman, I refused, knowing full well that his principal would go bananas and report me to the Attorney General, which everyone in the office would find very humorous. Thus it is ironic that the Stinchcombe name is forever enshrined in the principle of compulsory Crown disclosure.

Before *Stinchcombe*, full and fair disclosure, for example, witness statements, simply did not happen. It was a catch-22 situation, too, with most courts: if the defence had reason to believe that there might be a discrepancy or a contradiction between what the witness said to the police and what the witness was now saying on the stand, it was no use applying to the court for the production of the statement unless one could say what the contradiction was. But one could not say what the contradiction was, unless one consulted the statement. That was it for most judges: they simply ruled against the motion for production of the statements, without having to give reasons, when the Crown reared up on his hind legs and sanctimoniously asserted "these statements are the property of Her Majesty the Queen," whatever that meant, pompous and arrogant as it was. Well, one could only respond "to hell with you and rude letter to follow," but there was nothing much one could do about it.

So the bottom line was that pre-*Stinchcombe,* the defence never got witness statements – unless one had been around for a few years and was dealing with senior Crown counsel who were confident and trustworthy and many times the finest of fellows, and their daily practice would be to give you the Crown's entire file and point to the Xerox machine, and say "Well, now you will know as much about this case as I do." That happened.

Now, of course, what has evolved is that the defence gets everything including the reference booklet for the accused's kitchen stove. One gets not only the witness statements, but what the witness had for lunch last Thursday and the views of the witness' family on the Barcelona soccer team. That is, the defence is inundated with a plethora of paper. Much of this deluge might be irrelevant, but the defence counsel is obliged to comb through the entire package on the off chance that something relevant might present itself, just in case there was something in there that would help the hapless client however marginally, and for fear that in failing to do so the accused on appeal with another counsel will plead an incompetent defence at trial. It is a good time for a criminal trial lawyer to be out of practice.

In the days of hard copy, there were boxes of documents. Today, of course, all disclosure is by some sort of computer disk. There are cases where computer-illiterate lawyers have gone to the Court and demanded hard copy, but generally the Court sides with the Crown and says that this is the age of electronic miracles and the defence lawyer better buy himself some sort of computer and take some lessons.

Cases subsequent to *Stinchcombe* have clarified that if the material sought was apparently relevant and not in the hands of the Crown but being held by the police, the Crown still had the ethical duty to produce it. There were other cases dealing with relevant material, say for example medical mental records, in the hands of third parties not under the control of the Crown prosecutor. On a successful application for production the Court can order the third party agency to produce it to the defence, subject to protections.

In most jurisdictions, the Crown has its team of disclosure specialists who now provide the defence with the 'disclosure package', subject to defence undertakings regarding dissemination. Contested disclosure issues can arise pre-trial and mid-trial – and sometimes post trial – and can consume court time being litigated.

I must confess I much preferred the practice prior to the *Stinchcombe* ruling where, one's credibility being established with senior Crown prosecutors, one usually went to the prosecutor's office and the complete file of the Crown was shared with the defence without fuss. That was the way we did it in southern Alberta in the old days and it worked just fine.

Disclosure should be complete before the Accused elects to be tried by a judge and jury, a judge alone, or a provincial judge. *Stinchcombe* makes it clear that full and timely disclosure is essential to the progress and fairness of the criminal justice system. If not, adequate explanation must be provided by the Crown, because the accused is entitled to have a trial within a reasonable time, as are the victims of crime. I interject here the defence cynical precept in my day that "time runs in favor of the defence," that is, with the passage of time the Crown witnesses might die, preferably of natural causes.

In the recent revolutionary case of *R. v. Jordan*, a 5-4 decision, time limits to get to trial have now been set by the Supreme Court of Canada, citing sec. 11(b) of the *Charter*: eighteen months from charge to trial in Provincial Court; thirty months from charge to trial in Superior Courts, or criminal trial in Provincial Court after a preliminary inquiry. These time frames are subject to extension in appropriate circumstances. Defence delay does not count in the calculation. A strong dissent was written by Justice Thomas Cromwell, who argued that the new guidelines setting time lines for what constitutes unreasonable delay were "not an appropriate approach to interpreting and applying" the *Charter* right to a speedy trial, and that "creating fixed or presumptive ceilings is a task better left to legislatures."

An unwelcome development that has raised itself in recent days is the spectre of proposed 'defence disclosure' to the Crown in advance of the trial. What?! The one redoubt of the law where trial by ambush is still practiced is combat at the Criminal Bar. The very suggestion that there should be some sort of 'defence disclosure' to the Crown, because the Crown has the ethical duty to disclose to the defence, is outrageous to those of us who devoted our professional lives to the defence of persons accused of public crime. There were rare times during my practice when some judge importuned me to disclose 'the theory of the defence' at the pretrial or at some stage in the trial, to which my invariable reply was "Not proven." It is true that one was obliged to put the accused's version of the events in issue to the Crown witnesses, but it was usually absurd, and could hardly be justified with the moniker 'the defence theory'.

One of the innovative annoyances that surfaced at trial towards the last days of my practice was the attempt by some judges to have both the Crown and the defence assist him or her with the Court's charge to the jury, requiring both the Crown and defence to outline their 'theories' to the Court, preferably in a written submission, so they could be incorporated in the Court's charge. I refused to do this, stating that I had enough work to do on my own jury address, and the Court could do its own work. Further, there was no such animal as a 'defence theory'. This went over well, you can imagine, but as I have admonished fellow barristers, do not practice law on your knees!

When the spectre of defence disclosure raises its head, let us hark back to the rationale of criminal defence from the earliest days of the evolution of our Profession in 17th century England. It is a fashionable modern supposition among some judges and legal academics that a trial – civil or criminal – is a 'search for the truth'. That may hold some weight in civil disputes, but is nonsense in the criminal prosecution context. A criminal trial is not a search for the truth; it is a search for a result not incompatible with the truth. Neither dotty academics nor some ungifted judges can grasp this reality that is rooted in the immutable precepts that the accused is deemed to be innocent unless and until convicted by an impartial judge or jury on proof by the prosecutor to the requisite standard of guilt beyond a reasonable doubt. That should be the end of it, but it appears that the Alberta Court of Queen's Bench promulgated a 23-page 'pretrial conference report' suggesting defence disclosure well in advance of trial. That is, placing new burdens on the defence by back-dooring defence disclosure. Where that chapter ends, one does not know. I'm just as glad to be out of it.

7

THE JUDICIARY

*"I could never go to the Bench. It's not the loss of income,
it's the loss of prestige."*

*— My address to a plenary of the
National Criminal Law Program*

When I started practice, there were five Judges on the Supreme Court
Trial Division, all of whom had been top Barristers and Leaders of
the Bar. No lawyer with any brains or common sense elected trial by
jury in Alberta in those days. Indeed, it was worth your life to do so,
because Chief Justice McLaurin – who was brilliant and brief and
did not suffer fools and was usually right – had no tolerance whatsoever for juries. At the advent of my Call to the Bar, and for some
years after, one always had a choice in Alberta in a homicide case
to go by judge alone, and one always took it. Most homicides took
at most a couple of days, and no one thought anything of it. Now
the average homicide takes about eight to twelve weeks, the first
four or so weeks tied up in *Charter* applications seeking to exclude
evidence.

It was a great pleasure and a learning professional experience
to conduct a prosecution or defence before the Judges who were on
the Supreme Court Trial Division when I started practice. They were
courteous, crisp, no nonsense, learned in the law, "and minded to
keep it well." On more than one occasion I listened to a Judge say to

an accused felon: "As a man, Smith, I have no doubt that you did this reprehensible act. As a judge, on the evidence I am obliged to have a reasonable doubt. I find you not guilty." Mr. Justice Harold Riley, delivering this litany on one such occasion, paused at the judge's exit door, turned to the Accused, and said "You keep this up, Smith, you're going to be a dirty old man!" Pardon me for saying it: those were the days to practice criminal law.

Jury elections became fashionable at the Bar in Alberta due to some later woeful Bench appointments, some of the new appointees having no apparent concept of 'reasonable doubt', probably never having heard of it, nor of the precept that the accused is presumed to be innocent until proven guilty to the requisite standard, that is, beyond all reasonable doubt. One elected trial by jury to escape judges who had never practiced at the trial bar. In the old days, we could always do a last minute dump, usually going to see the Chief Justice or an Assigning Judge with a list of five judges that we would be happy to go before by judge alone. The Crown would often say they took no part in 'Judge picking', so the Assigning Judge would simply ignore the prosecution and ask the defence, "Who do you want?" That worked pretty well.

I took quite a few juries over the years, usually in cases that looked absolutely hopeless and one could hope that at least one of twelve *National Enquirer* readers might cut the accused loose. In particular, one seasoned Judge called the Crown and me to his Chambers before trial, and asked me "Why are you going with a jury? I'm a reasonable guy, and I can have a reasonable doubt." To which I responded, "Even you would convict this sonofabitch." After the jury convicted, he looked at me and said "I see what you mean." In any criminal case, after the Judge charged the jury, it was standard practice for counsel to go to the Judge's chambers and quaff a few civilized drinks while waiting for the verdict. That practice is now completely *verboten*. New judges are horrified at the suggestion that they might be criticized by the press or a party for enjoying a social professional visit with experienced counsel.

At the fifty-year mark, I no longer enjoyed the practice of law.

• • •

Of historical note, some significant revolutionary developments and reforms were instituted in the reconstitution and structuring of Alberta courts during my practice. These were entirely appropriate, and long overdue. At the low end of the scale was the Magistrates' Court, commonly known as Police Court, whose judges did not need to be legally trained and were addressed as "your Worship." The Provincial Court of Alberta – rising like the Phoenix from the ashes of the Magistrates Court/the Police Court – now became a Court of Record, the Judges to wear distinctive blue-trimmed gowns and to be addressed as "Your Honour." As one Honourable Provincial Judge observed, this innovation was somewhat of a come down: one having formerly worshiped them, now one merely honoured them. Magistrates could retain the honorific of Queen's Counsel, but such distinctions were no longer attached to provincial judges, although the ascent to the outer ether was said to be a promotion. The really big initiative rammed through by the Attorney General of Alberta of the day, Jim Foster QC, circa 1974, with the blessing of the Premier, was the change of name and dress and complete restructuring of the Trial Division of the Supreme Court of Alberta, as it was then named, which was literally squished with the District Court of Northern and Southern Alberta to become the Court of Queen's Bench of Alberta.

A delightful contemporary criticism of the squishing process by Chief Justice Milvain of the then Trial Division greatly appealed to me, highlighting notorious facts that some of the judicial appointees to the Alberta District Court of that era were neither legal rocket scientists nor well-connected. The District Court became a bit of a boneyard for some opportunists aspiring to the Supreme Court but falling short of the requisite moxy or leverage in the old boy network of the day. Thus the late great Chief Justice, long my mentor and friend, told me over a glass or two of his celebrated Vat 69 whiskey that he had remonstrated with the Attorney General: "I said to him, what about the turkey factor?" I loved that line.

That said, there were in my day some really sound judges on the

District Court. The District Court was reasonably useful in that one could appeal a summary conviction and get a hearing called a Trial *de Novo* – literally, a new trial, but in the higher Court – in a reasonable time. The District Court also presided in criminal trials – the 'speedy trial'– falling short of intentional homicide, that is, murder, but did not preside with Juries.

A couple of years later when I was on the Benchers and attending convocation, I was advised that there was a long-distance call for me. I took the call, because it was from a Justice of another jurisdiction who had always been a valued professional colleague, having been a top partner of a large legal firm and now a very senior judge. He advised me that he was dealing with the proposed amalgamation of his province's version of our late District Court with their Supreme Court, and did I have any helpful comments. I said to him, "What about the turkey factor?" He also loved that line.

In our shakeup process, the Appellate Division of the Supreme Court of Alberta became the Alberta Court of Appeal, which Court celebrated in 2014 its hundredth anniversary with soporific dinners in Edmonton and Calgary. With some reluctance, I dragged myself to the Calgary scene, and it turned out to be as dreadful as I had feared. The guest speaker was the renowned constitutional fundamentalist Justice Antonin Scalia of the US Supreme Court. There were about 750 judges and lawyers crammed into the Westin banquet hall, and one had to empathize with the late Justice Scalia as he was preceded by no less than seven other speakers, most of them deadly boring and completely unnecessary. I have treated of this debacle in my later chapter in this book on the decline of the no-holds-barred Bar social function, another casualty of the revolution.

There was a great deal of animosity and engineered opposition to the proposed amalgamation and streamlining of the high courts in Alberta, which I confess I found surprising as coming from the Bar as well as coming from other judges. Naturally, it was opposed, sometimes vociferously, by current appointees to the then Supreme Court Trial Division, who valued their turf and did not welcome outsiders.

One story surfaced of the comment by one senior Justice, a former redoubtable and formidable barrister, when asked what colour gown he would wear as the Queen's Bench was to have new fancy red trim, responded "I shall wear only black."

As I recall, the former Attorney General had to contend not only with recalcitrant opposing Judiciary but also senior members of the Bar, in particular, several of the elected Benchers of the day, who were 'elected', it will be remembered, by the big firm loaded practice of which I have written elsewhere in this book. It will also be remembered, apropos of my other comments in this book, that the old boy network still ran our Profession in Alberta until it was itself run out in the early 1980s *et seq.* The plain fact is that the so-called Leaders of the Bar who were the governors of the Law Society were also charter members of exclusive private clubs where they hobnobbed with the High Court judges. One would not be surprised that it was in such distinguished repositories that opposition to the Attorney General's initiative was hatched and fomented.

However, it also became quite clear that the majority of the Bar were in favour of the amalgamation, and wearied of the invocations and paranoid concerns of the Old Boys which were ultimately ignored, and that was that. One cannot halt progress because one is nostalgic for the habitual and customary oppressions of the old days. On balance, from the point of view of members of the Bar who were in favor of the Attorney General's courageous innovation, to borrow a delightful aphorism, the amalgamation of the District Court of Alberta with the Supreme Court Trial Division raised the mean IQ of both courts. Lawyers always take themselves too seriously. Commenting on his elevation to the Court of Appeal at his swearing in, the always-witty Justice McClung noted "It's inside work and there's no heavy lifting."

• • •

I have always embraced George Orwell's classic description in *England Your England* of the austere incorruptible English judge who knew the law and kept it well as "one of the symbolic figures of England."

Director Billy Wilder's *Witness for the Prosecution*, starring the brilliant Charles Laughton playing the redoubtable English Queen's Counsel known as Wilfred the Fox, remains one of my favourite films, no doubt because it portrayed the historic English Court and the challenges as well as the courtesies of the Barristers' profession, which have somehow become dimmed and now lost in the course of the fifty-year revolution in the legal profession. The opening of the film is a dramatic portrait of the impartial and severe British Court of Queen's Bench: the Red Judge, robed in the manner of a Renaissance Pope, enters as the Clerk of the Court intones "Be upstanding!" No one would dare to be downstanding. The Judge stands before his raised seat, bows to gowned and wigged counsel who, in turn, return his bow, and the Clerk proclaims: *"Oyez Oyez Oyez!* All those having matters before this Court of Oyer and Terminer come forward, and you shall be heard."

Magnificent echoes there of *Magna Carta*: "We shall appoint as judges only those who know the law and are minded to keep it well."

What a nostalgic milieu, now vanished, swallowed up in the sheer volume of cases and the relentless demands on judicial time. The Guildhalls! Peter Cook in his celebrated *Beyond the Fringe* sketch, circa 1960, had it right: "I would rather be a judge than a miner. There's not much coal falling in the guildhalls."

I have spent a lot of my professional life trying to keep at arms-length from the judiciary, and have emphatically refused any opportunities to go to the Bench, but I am still mired in contact with judges because eight of my law partners over the years could not withstand the powerful temptation to have people stand and genuflect when they entered the courtroom.

It is grade-school conventional wisdom that the linchpin separation of powers in a democratic polity are the legislative, the executive, and the judiciary. That necessarily said, it was always axiomatic to conclude that in Canada, the judiciary was independent. An independent judiciary, presiding in a fair and impartial tribunal, is paramount in a free and democratic society.

As to whether individual judges are 'objective' and 'fair', those requisites are regrettably subject to personal biases, prejudices, snobbery, or incompetence. A big leg up for the biased and incompetent was the penchant of the recently dumped federal Conservative oligarchy to build more jails and jail more accused persons. This brought in the 'tough-on-crime' legislation of mandatory minimum sentences for any number of offenses where surely the weighing of aggravating and mitigating factors should be left to the presiding judge. The new laws purported to bind the judiciary to impose minimal jail sentences on conviction of an accused person for specific delicts.

A judge has an obligation to weigh scrupulously the aggravating and mitigating factors in the sentencing process. The judge must have, subject to guidance from higher courts that are binding upon her/him, complete freedom of thought and conscience in arriving at what his/her discretion concludes to be an appropriate sentence for an accused person. The judge must be cognizant of, and must apply, the 'starting points' articulated by Courts of Appeal and the Supreme Court of Canada for specific offences, and to factor these guidelines into the overall consideration of the instant case. Notwithstanding the significance of 'starting points', there are always exceptional cases where the corroborated mitigating factors are of such magnitude as to mandate mercy, and in the rarest case the fashioning of the sentence below legislative minimum upon application of the Charter proscription against 'cruel and unusual punishment'.

Where a political party controlling a legislative body, purporting to be acting in the best interest of the citizens but with the true and devious purpose of currying – i.e. purchasing – voter favour, promotes and implements oppressive legislation affecting the independence of the judiciary and the entitlement of the accused citizen to the objective judgment of a court of law, the freedoms of Canada are at an end.

There is no place for the squeamish in this debate. Interference with and curtailment of the exercise of judicial discretion is totalitarianism.

• • •

Edmund Burke commented on the revolutionary legislators of the National Assembly of France in his *Reflections on the Revolution in France*. He charged that a majority of the Assembly was composed of undistinguished practitioners in the law, who were previously neither prudent magistrates nor leading advocates nor renowned professors, but for the greater part inferior and unlearned. He adds "There were distinguished exceptions…"

He is critical of some members, previously of subordinate station, suddenly invested with authority which they would be surprised to have attained. He was concerned that they could not be expected to bear with equanimity, or to conduct with sound judgment, this new power.

Just substitute "some Judges" for "revolutionary legislators in the National Assembly of France." The ranks of the judiciary – with some distinguished exceptions – are infiltrated, to some proportion, by *arrivistes* who are wanting in sagacity and compassion or are otherwise not qualified to sit in judgment on others

A daunting concern of the Criminal Bar in particular is ensuring judicial independence from rampant political correctness. A Calgary defence counsel quite recently was asked to comment on the acquittal of his client by a different judge in a second trial. Comments made by the judge in the course of the first trial ending in a judgment of acquittal came under heavy fire and indeed national criticism and complaints resulting in a lengthy hearing before a Canadian Judicial Council Inquiry panel. He had acquitted the accused in the first trial, having in its course made some inappropriate offensive remarks. The Alberta Court of Appeal in setting aside the acquittal and ordering a new trial had "doubts about the trial judge's understanding" of the law applicable to sexual assault.

When asked about the conduct of the first trial judge, the defence counsel reflected eloquently: "…Would you rather have your judge make the right decision and say something inappropriate, or be politically correct and get the wrong decision?"

Commenting on the situation, the eminent Christie Blatchford wrote in the *National Post*, Saturday, February 4, 2017 that the threat raised by the lawyer in the case referred to is "real and increasingly pervasive."

As recently as a few months ago, Reid Fiest, a Global News national Alberta correspondent observed that, while many judicial appointees had some life experience, their legal experience was not in criminal law. The writer concluded that the majority of federal judges do not have significant criminal law experience, stating that only about one third of those named to Alberta's Court of Queen's Bench in the last five years had practiced criminal or family law. He pointed out that the majority of the cases heard by the Court are criminal or family in nature. Further, at the time of his writing, there were over fifty vacant positions across Canada, leading to big trial delays. Responding to this criticism, my great and good friend the former Chief Justice of the Court of Queen's Bench of Alberta, Allan Wachowich, said the judge's background was not an issue. He said that judicial appointees have to have general experience: "Usually judges who are good lawyers, or have the reputation to be good lawyers, can adapt to this system." Allan Wachowich was one of the finest trial judges I have argued major cases before, and I have the greatest respect for him and his views.

I suppose I can be tolerant of some of Her Majesty's Judges if they have never heard of Erskine or Carson or Lord Brougham, but it is too much for me that one who has never in practice conducted a criminal trial of a serious charge for the Crown or defence is presiding with a Jury on major homicide cases.

• • •

Appointments to The Bench? Eight of my partners over forty-five years have taken the judicial ermine. I distinctly remember two identical admonitions, one to me by a High Court Judge; the other to a friend, the senior partner in a major law firm, by a

Court of Appeal justice: "Why don't you come up here with us?" This query contained its own major premise, thus proving that there was influence to be had in high places. I knew this to be fallacious. The cold truth is that the real influence is to be had in low places.

One is at once placed in mind of the more recent judicial appointments processes, both federal and provincial, which include the obligatory "What I did on my summer holiday" type questions. If I get the proverbial dollar for every applicant who answers the question "Why do you want to be a judge" with the sophomoric, hypocritical bromide: "I want to give back to the community, etc.", I would be the proverbial millionaire. And one has to appear in front of some of these nincompoops.

A.D. Hunter QC, President of the Law Society, observed that the holding out of "an appointment" was "a powerful appeal to the vanities, and hard to resist." I appeared before him and the assembled Benchers "in convocation" on behalf of a Judge who had resigned after a short term of appointment, and wanted to go back to the Bar. Hunter pontificated: "Those who would seek and embrace, enjoy and abuse the usufructs, emoluments and privileges of high office cannot simply return to practice without an appropriate sanction." In other words, there would be a waiting period before one could appear before the Court on which one had sat. (On other occasions, Alan had great lines like "We have no cause to be sanguine..." and "He resiled upon his commitment...", that sort of thing.) Case in point was my old and dear friend, a distinguished counsel of Vancouver. A leading criminal lawyer of his day, he was appointed to the Supreme Court of British Columbia. He resigned from the Bench after seven years service. The B.C. Benchers ruled that he could not appear before the Supreme Court or the Provincial Court as an advocate for one-and-a-half years, having promulgated a rule to delay a former judge from appearing before his contemporaries.

It is noteworthy that female justices of the high courts, federal appointments, have an annual fish fry and purloo in Ottawa, all expenses paid. The male judges have no such event. So much for 'diversity'. One is reminded of the Alberta female Justices petition to the Federal Pension Commission regarding the pensions of female high court judges, couched as a gender inequality issue. As I recall, there were nine signatories to the petition. The submission – that it was a 'gender inequality issue' – caused demurrers of derision, even from such feminist supporters as a well-respected national newspaper columnist. The point of the submission was that women had given up significant positions in practice to become judges, and had made sacrifices financially to do so. This was a bit much. Other than the exceptions of two of the petitioners I can name, for most of the female appointees to the High Court the appointment was like winning the lottery or inheriting a producing goldmine. Mind you, the puling of a lot of judges of all Courts about the parsimonious perquisites and stingy emoluments of their offices and the financial sacrifices they have made in taking an appointment is a constant, tedious refrain of sniveling and whining. They make damn good money. On top of this, they get genuflecting for free.

8

IMPACT OF THE COMPUTER

"We are all living in science fiction right now.
Our world would have been unimaginable to people
fifty years ago or a hundred years ago."

— *Elan Mastai, quoted in Saturday February 11, 2017 National Post*

This chapter reflects upon the truly revolutionary impact of the computer and the cell phone – 'personal digital devices' – on the practice of law. For the first thirty-five years of my practice no one had a computer and no one had a cell phone. Day-to-day legal business was transacted between professional colleagues who trusted each other – by far the majority in practice, save for the very few whose word could not be trusted – in the usual manner: a phone discussion or a meeting and a handshake; you said you would do something, and when the day came to do it, you did it. In the late 1980s, one started to see a tendency in junior lawyers to exchange insulting letters, say, following an examination for discovery, wherein they would demand production of that which had already been agreed to. But these were somewhat of an exception. It was just not the practice to write screeds to the other side: one did what had to be done, whether a commercial transaction, a real estate deal, or a litigation, or for that matter a criminal case. With the advent of email one was inundated daily with cryptic communications from the other side, usually requiring a response.

And one spoke on the telephone to one's learned friend as a matter of course. Today, it does not appear that anyone utilizes the telephone, either to contact someone or to respond to a caller. Everything is done by text or email. The only prejudicial evidentiary concomitant that few members of the public appear to understand or appreciate is that emails and texts, even if purportedly erased, can easily be resurrected either via a computer geek or by a subpoena to the server: that is, the supposedly private and sometimes embarrassing communications that one thought were expunged all of a sudden can be rounded up and have to be disclosed in all civil litigation, and frequently put in evidence by the Crown in criminal litigation. That is enough to scare one off either form of communication other than a restaurant reservation or an innocent appointment to meet a friend for a drink.

One harks back to the Saturday, December 30, 1989 edition of *The Globe and Mail* newspaper to which I referred in my introductory chapters. It features an excellent article on the impact of modern technology, including computers, by Mary Gooderham, who wrote about applied science for the newspaper. She ends with the admonition of Marshall McLuhan that the technological culture has insulated people from their fellows. "The world is shrinking, and many humans, it seems, want less and less to do with it." She notes that technology has swallowed us up as machines threatened to become things we could not do without. On the computer's emergence in the 1980s she observes that 'the revolution' got under way with the availability to all of affordable, manageable, personal computers. Universal access to information technology dramatically changed the business environment.

With the advent of the computer, Crown disclosure usually came by way of a DVD disc, loaded with all or any data possibly related to the instant case, including how many cars were driven through the criminal venue between certain hours and the contents of the dead person's child's toybox. The problem that was created is that one had to go through absolutely everything, just in case, hidden somewhere in that plethora of information, there was something relevant to the defence. Failure to do so might result in an application to the appeal court citing defence counsel for incompetence. (See *Chapter 6.*)

The Cellphone

The most potent instrument of unrequitement in this modern world is the ubiquitous cell phone, its 'apps' now including e-mail and texting. It is an era of instantaneous communication, even across borders and over great distances. Thus, if one transmits, that is, 'sends a text' and one does not hear positive feedback, or one does not hear back at all, these are crushing rejections, and prequels to depression. Because if the textee shares with every other human blank the ability to respond to such communications instanter, utilizing a similar instrument, and does not, then it is a reasonable conclusion that one's message – and one – have been ignored. Swift opined that indifference was by far the worst treatment of another human being.

I sit, hunched, waiting for the 'ping' of my phone that tells me I have a response to my latest sally. No ping. Unrequitement.

All of which resurrects my generalization about the habitual denizens of the Eighth Avenue Mall and the blight of the cellphone. Speaking of revolutions, Calgary has grown exponentially from the 100,000 population on my arrival in 1948 to over one million circa 2017. I am striding down the mall, confirming my five categories of *homo sapiens sapiens*: beggars and mooches, some genuinely down and out and filthy and lice ridden and disreputable and homeless, but most are professionals, each with his/her own territory; every third person is morbidly obese; there are the usual botched with the staggers and jags, wasted by street drugs laced with additives or afflicted with Tourette's Syndrome or bipolar or hypomanic, and just screaming obscenities or something unintelligible; young guys in packs like wolves, trolling for females, occupying most of the sidewalk café summer seating, guzzling beer, as no one seems to work anymore on a weekday; and the odd ordinary person like myself. Very odd.

One thing that is a constant: everybody has a cell phone, and easily four out of five adults or children in any place at any time are anxiously consulting these hateful instruments. What all of these people have in common, each and every one, is his/her cellphone. This ubiquitous, indeed iniquitous instrument is now the apparent centrepiece of all human intercourse and commerce, thus is much or more in evidence in every vacant-eyed user's hand. Everybody has a cell phone: at all material times with some, and frequent intervals with others, there is the frowning scanning, dialing, texting, checking one's personal advertising with one's social media sites, and chatting, chatting, chatting, delivered at importunistic decibels: "I says to him and he says to me and I says and he says and I sez and my ma sez…" and "I'm like and she's like and he's like and, like, like…"

What sums up the *raison d'être* of the average person is that her and his sole prodigious efforts – when not devoted to an exchange of unsolicited autobiographical information and grunted mutual ignorances – are directed to the cellphone's delights, so extensive now that there is about a million times more data stashed on the average cellphone than on the modified improved IBM computer of 1945 which filled an entire twelve story building, and one can now check the temperature of ones's oven and the fortunes of the Barcelona soccer team and, if one has some rudimentary hacker skills which all young people appear these days to be born with, one can hack into someone else's private life with alacrity.

Thus the writer, sashaying down the mall, notes almost every person is apparently glued to a cellphone, texting perfervidly or talking loudly and ostentatiously; some blithering fools are sporting a headset and carrying on at intense decibels a banal conversation; and also as observed, every third person is obese as well as fastened to a cell phone.

Late of an evening, one perhaps peckish repairs to a popular late night restaurant in the trendy district. At the typical table are six to eight young people all talking to or consulting their cell phone or texting, oblivious to their companions. The suggestion that devices of this nature have improved the communication of the species is absurd: an exchange of grunts or the emitting of a musical yelp by a denizen of the Stone Age would yield more human contact. Today's models of phones, heavily competitive, in addition to the usual functions, offer videos of just about everything in the entertainment universe, the closing price of molybdenum on the Eurasian commodities market, the photographs taken by your ex and loaded onto the Internet, and an e-mail message from your boss that you're fired. But you cannot get Philip Larkin reading *Vers de Societe*: not good for sales. What sells phones is the promise of a plethora of useless information that one cannot live without.

The phenomenon that a people ostensibly so free could in fact be so enslaved would be curious if it were not banal. In the evenings, all the occupants are glued to the blue emanations of the goggle box, searching for the bolt of lightning prefacing the peal of thunder. Sound, flashing colour, few second sound bites, rat-a-tat commercials.

My considered opinion has been reduced to this monograph upon the subject, wherein the tiny like-minded enlightened minority are denounced as Luddites and sent to Coventry, which today involves being stripped of one's cell phone. A sound reason to plead guilty and to be sentenced to read Gibbon or Edmund Burke or Proust in perpetuity.

Social Media

I freely confess that the whole concept of so-called 'social media' fills me with revulsion and distaste. I am a very private person, in my dotage practically reclusive, and the wholesale delivery of their private lives to complete strangers by the vast majority of populations even in failed states and third world countries strikes me as completely absurd. Why I should wish to scroll daily through my social media network feed to see if a cousin for whom I care nothing has posted a DVD of her pet salamander or I have been 'tagged' by a relative in an inspirational quote or there is a request 'pop-up' or status updates or even embarrassing photos is quite beyond me for any aspiration that I might have. Much has been made as at this writing of the new US President's alarming penchant to post daily absurdities on something called Twitter. Again, this is free confession not made under torture or by inducement: I have no idea what Twitter is, and I do not wish to find out. Nor do I want to be briefed on what is called 'outing' by online communications or something going 'viral'. I have not the slightest idea what these things are, and I make no apology for it. I gave up watching television a number of years ago and got a third of my life back. I am not prepared to give three quarters of my life to intimate social network communications.

In July 2014 in Halifax, I attended a National Criminal Law Program panel discussing lawyers and social media. The general import of the panel was that it was not wise for practicing lawyers to go on social media networks, certainly not to discuss her or his cases, nor to suffer hits and postings and 'dislikes' from those seeking to discredit the lawyer. Presumably, it is not inappropriate for a lawyer to join a social network designated for professional relationships, although one gets weary of being inundated by emails stating that so-and-so has invited one to be posted as a friend or business associate on their business site. No thank you.

I had the opportunity to review the papers prepared for that program by a leading justice, a leader of the criminal bar, and a distinguished professor of law. In the context of social media, they were discussing social media practices and law-enforcement; pretrial publicity; and the open court principle.

The reasonable expectation of privacy

Dealing with the first, social media and law-enforcement, how can Canadian citizens purport to preserve their 'essential' privacy when they voluntarily subscribe to social media, willingly sharing vast amounts of highly personal information with others, including strangers? Our private lives, not that long ago, were private; now they our public.

Social media networks are a cornucopia of evidence for investigators and prosecutors, as well as providing information to defence counsel. In addition, they are a new forum for the commission of criminal activity, which I will talk about later in this discussion.

Dealing with the first of these, the use by law enforcement of social media intelligence raises privacy concerns. Does one have a reasonable expectation of privacy when one sends an email or a text? Section 8 of the *Charter* protects to some extent the right to remain private in public spaces. The trend in the US appears to be that once one sends a text or an email, they are in the public domain; Courts in Canada are starting to take a more restrictive approach, applying section 8 of the Charter, holding that in certain circumstances the text or email author may have a reasonable expectation of privacy and therefore a specific judicial warrant was necessary in order to monitor and collect these communications.

The Ontario Court of Appeal noted that a person "by allowing others into a zone of personal privacy, does not forfeit the claim that the state is excluded from that zone of privacy." Are reasonable and informed Canadians going to recognize the existence of a constitutionally protected privacy interest? One has to look at the context, and whether the communication was intended to be public or private. Practicing criminal lawyers as well as legal scholars and judges are currently wrestling with *Charter* and legal questions raised by 'personal digital devices' such as computers and cell phones being seized and searched by the police. In particular, the point is argued that privacy interests at stake in computer searches and searches of electronically stored data are different from those at stake in searches of physical spaces. There is also the live issue of whether an ensuing search by the investigating authority after warrantless seizure could be said to be 'incidental to the arrest'. So there is a lot of work for my colleagues out there in digital data land.

The bottom line is that social networking sites are potentially fruitful sources of evidence for law enforcement, but the admissibility of this evidence will be countered by the raising of privacy concerns.

Social media is also an opportunity for bullies. This raises the question of the reasonable expectation of privacy, because one does not necessarily consent to the distribution on the Internet of one's photographs given in confidence to another person. Social media can also be employed for indecent or harassing communications. Online bullying using social media is "an enormously complex problem" says one expert.

Social Media and the Open Courts Principle

Pretrial publicity is particularly challenged by social media. Social media is Internet based, meaning the information can reach a global audience and is impossible to control once released; social media is interactive and has the ability for live multi-party communication between any individuals situated anywhere. Pretrial publicity, dealing with tainting of impartiality of the jury by publicly available information, gets bogged down in a whole new area: the spread of information and the fact that anyone can broadcast it.

Before the proliferation of social media, a publication ban by the court was usually reliable enough to keep a jury unaware of the worst aspects. The Internet has eroded this: bans issued to maintain jury impartiality do not work that well anymore. Publication bans have little hope of controlling the flow of information into the jury pool. Whereas a responsible journalist adheres to publication bans, there is no restraint on any person in the courtroom audience from texting to an outsider the name of a protected witness or of the victim. Any member of the jury can send a text to anyone out there about what is going on in the courtroom, and receive a text advising of something deleterious to the accused person they are trying. A judicial colleague of mine was aghast at the number of jurors sitting as triers of fact in a serious criminal case who were actively deploying cell phones throughout! The result, an undesirable expedient: more closed courts.

More and more sensitive aspects of the court proceedings may have to be held in camera, which goes against the principle enunciated so well by the late Chief Justice Samuel Friedman of Manitoba: "Publicity is the hallmark of a judicial inquiry."

As for the application for a change of venue, whereas one might wish to leave one municipal area where the crime is allegedly notorious for some other place where nobody is likely to have heard of it, that is all changed with the advent of social media. Bottom line: social media has the capability to almost instantly prejudice a wide swath of the public. This puts a heavy burden on defence counsel who will be increasingly challenged and frustrated in their efforts to protect their client's interests in the face of the Internet and social media and unsupervised instant communication.

Advocates of social media preach that social networking sites allow the younger generation to express themselves and share their experiences and mingle democratically with multitudes from all strata of society. I suppose that is all well and good for a younger generation that does not share my devotion to privacy, not to mention that many a callow youth is propagandized and sometimes radicalized by Internet manipulators.

I confess to being an Internet layman and a computer illiterate. One reads that experts can glean all sorts of private information from searching the Internet about one who is a devotee of social media. It is reported that in a very short time, they can produce heaps of profoundly private and invasive personal information supposed to have been visible only to the subject's 'friends' on the networking websites.

If that is not enough to give one pause, one learns that criminals are using a person's private information disseminated on the Internet to that person's detriment in ways that one cannot anticipate. They have devised sophisticated ways to target unsophisticated victims: they can burgle one's homes; obtain one's bank and credit card details; added to that information, they can obtain particulars of residence, employment, and relationships, and use one's identity to commit fraud or theft or to tailor a scam using private details to lure one into the scheme. Well, lots more custom for criminal defence counsel.

I should think if a criminal lawyer is addicted to his or her social media feed, he or she will need to consider everything he/she types, posts, shares and uploads. One must check, for example, the security of one's profile to know what other people can see. What you once thought was private might have become public. In sum, I fail to see how any person can claim to have 3,752 'friends' and never have met any of them. Some of them may not be friendly. That settles it. If I want a friend, I'll buy a dog.

Acknowledgments for source material for previous chapter:

December 30, 1989 edition of *The Globe and Mail* newspaper. Three papers prepared for the Federation of Law Societies National Criminal Law Program, Halifax, Nova Scotia, July, 2014:

"Privacy as an Elusive Hare: Social Media, Social Practices and Law Enforcement," by the Hon. Justice Gregory J Fitch.

"Social Media and Pretrial Publicity," by Scott C. Hutchison

"Social Media and the Open Courts Principle," by Prof. Robert Currie.

9

THE DECLINE OF ADVOCACY

*"An advocate, in the discharge of his duty, knows but
one person in all the world, and that person is his client.
To save that client by all means and expedients, and at all hazards and
costs to other persons, and, amongst them, to himself, is his
first and only duty; and in performing this duty he must not
regard the alarm, the torments, the destruction which
he may bring upon others. Separating the duty of a patriot
from that of an advocate, he must go on reckless
of the consequences, though it should be his unhappy fate to
involve his country in confusion."*

— Lord Brougham in Queen Caroline's Case, 1820

That famous admonition from a great barrister, together with Thomas Erskine's classic address to the jury in the case of Thomas Paine (which is set out in my Introduction), should be force-fed to every first year law student in this country. Erskine postulated that the barrister requested to undertake a brief on behalf of an accused client, however disreputable in the public or indeed the professional purview, has a sacred duty to undertake that defence,

I have essentially two additional admonitions to prospective barristers:

(1) Keep your word. You will either practice honourably, or you will be dishonourable. In the latter case, the profession will quickly learn that your word is not to be trusted. Simply adhere to the address of Thomas Mowbray to *Richard the Second*, Act 1, Scene 1:

> The purest treasure mortal times afford is spotless reputa-
> tion: that away, Men are but gilded loam or painted clay…
> Mine honour is my life; both grow in one: Take honour from
> me, and my life is done…"

Correspondence to the Editor in the Spring 2017 *Journal of the American College of Trial Lawyers* quoted Lord Neuberger, President of the Supreme Court of the United Kingdom, speaking on legal ethics in the 21st Century: "Together with judges, lawyers are the quintessential representatives, or ambassadors, of the rule of law so far as the general public is concerned… If lawyers and judges are not competent and honest… the rule of law is severely undermined."

(2) The second admonition is simple: Do not practice law on your knees! Regrettably, as part of the more tedious baggage accompanying the revolution in my profession, Lord Brougham's admonition, the perspective that the duty owed by a lawyer to his or her client was paramount over all others, is giving way in Canada to the prevailing view that it is not consistent with something labeled 'lawyer professionalism', that is, the duty to clients must co-exist with several other 'duties', e.g. to the public, to the Courts, to witnesses, to colleagues, to the Profession. So one pleads the client guilty to save the Court's time and the taxpayers' money and spare the witnesses?

No barrister worth his or her gown, in defending a person charged with public crime in this country, can water down zealous advocacy as the important element in fulfilling the duty of representing the client's interests. Barristers must be entitled to freedom of expression in the Courtroom to make full answer and defence in a criminal case and to present their position in a civil case. The promulgation of rules of conduct to demote trial counsel to sycophants is probably by those who have never conducted a criminal trial of serious charges for the prosecution or for the defence, and live in cloud cuckoo land. Having been at this game for fifty years, on my feet in every level of courtroom in this country, I have neither time nor patience for the 'gentle' approach to advocacy. As I have said, it is currently fashionable, one of the more absurd concomitants of the revolution. The 'gentle approach' to the conduct of a civil or criminal trial has gained considerable currency at law schools and legal education outfits, none of whom appreciate any concept of brawling on one's feet, blood on the floor, in the courtroom. A trial – criminal or civil – is combat, pure and simple. The object is to win, not kiss your opponent's fundament. In winning, the object is to put the other side to the floor. But remember always, please, to be 'civil': there is magnanimity in victory. Victors write the history.

I read a recent newspaper report that prominent Ontario barrister Earl Cherniak QC was representing a lawyer on his appeal to the Supreme Court of Canada from a split decision of the Ontario Court of Appeal upholding the findings of a Law Society of Upper Canada discipline panel as corroborated by an appeal panel, to the effect that the lawyer was allegedly too aggressive in his defence of a client in Court. The Supreme Court has granted leave to appeal. As the case is under judicial consideration at this writing, I cannot make any comment upon the issues currently before the Supreme Court. The *sub judice* rule limits the public statements that can be made about ongoing legal proceedings before the courts.

There is a special poignancy to this story, because I have always had great respect for, and a unique professional friendship with, the brilliant barrister Earl Cherniak QC, a Leader of the Bar for decades and known far and wide as the Dean of Canadian tort lawyers. In the early 1980s, I was Called to the Bar in Ontario for the purpose of defending a long and complicated alleged fraud prosecution over two years of preliminary inquiry and six week trial, ending in the acquittal of my client. I have written of this case in *A Painful Duty*. Shortly after I put up at a Toronto hotel with the preliminary inquiry commencing the next day in Old City Hall, I received a telephone call from Earl Cherniak QC wishing me a warm welcome to the Ontario Bar. I shall always remember his gracious gesture of the old style of professional camaraderie that existed in our profession in days gone by.

I was asked a couple of times to take part as guest faculty at the Legal Education Society of Alberta's annual 'Advanced Advocacy' course at the University of Calgary in June. My recollection is I participated in two of these week-long exercises, contributing two days as a guest instructor. This included my doing demonstrations of cross-examinations and jury addresses at plenary sessions. It is noteworthy that the barristers who did the plenary demos were often experienced criminal lawyers. The faculty was composed mostly of civil trial lawyers, a couple of judges, and three or four criminal lawyers.

Most of the registrants, who averaged four or five years at the Bar and were seeking to improve their courtroom skills, were usually employed in civil litigation mills and were therefore not novices or students. There were very few criminal lawyers registered: out of, say, fifty registrants, two or three at the most might be criminal lawyers. Nevertheless, they were all there to learn, and had paid a fee to learn, one presumes, the recondite secrets of aggressive advocacy. Advocacy can be aggressive but it does not have to be unethical. Anyone with half a loaf knows that. I was asked again recently to participate as faculty, but I declined.

I was really put off by the admonition of a Judge, a fine fellow and otherwise exemplary judge, to the plenary session that the sole desirable object of trial advocacy was the objective pursuit of "the proper administration of justice." What nonsense! The object of effective trial advocacy is to win the case.

At a teaching session with eight students practicing examination-in- chief and cross-examination under the coaching of a faculty member and myself, I was absolutely astonished when my teaching partner – who was an able trial lawyer – admonished the students that "In cross-examination, 'I put it to you' is a no-no." What? It was apparently not polite to the witness! And to call it a "no-no", as if lecturing grade threes! I said at once that I completely disagreed with my colleague, that the affirmative cross question "I put it to you" was a classic in constant use by opposing counsel in criminal trials, and then and there I gave the class an example (which ticked off my teaching partner):

> Mr. Evans: I put it to you that your story is a tissue of fabrications.
>
> The Crown Witness: Huh?
>
> Mr. Evans: You're a damn liar.
>
> The Judge: You've gone too far with that one, Counsel.
>
> Mr. Evans: I did it and I'm glad.

If advocacy coaches are going to continue to teach aspiring trial lawyers that they must first and foremost, on their feet in the court-room, be Ms. or Mr. Congeniality, I regret that I shall have nothing more to contribute to their programs. At least, so far, the National Criminal Law Program (Canada) has not adopted this veneer of 'kindly' advocacy as opposed to the duty of zealous representation.

That is not to suggest that congeniality and civility should not be pursued in one's day-to-day encounters with colleagues and members of the public. Professional courtesy and civility particularly between trial counsel, a long-standing tradition, today is observed more in the breach than in the performance. Too many young lawyers appear to get cranked like sausages out of the law schools with no concept of this obligation.

One of the points I should like to make is the mutual camaraderie that often develops in the course of a trial where opposing counsel are professional, courteous and competent and the Judge that presides is evenhanded, able, and experienced. That was the case with several challenging trials in the course of my career, more so because it was encouraged and enhanced by the generally poison courtroom atmosphere engendered by the attendance of the understandably greatly bereaved and vocal relatives of the alleged victim, sometimes dead.

Advocacy is the art of persuasion, but it is a dying art. Whereas Erskine KC and his contemporaries habitually addressed juries sometimes for hours, or made equally lengthy arguments before judges, most courts of appeal now impose strict time limits so that one has only a few minutes to make one's point, however complicated or difficult or innovative, suffering frequent interruptions and questions from the court.

Barristers in other Commonwealth jurisdictions literally for centuries enjoyed exclusive access to the high courts. There was a huge uproar in the United Kingdom in – as I recall – the late 80s, when the first solicitor was appointed Queen's Counsel, and the first solicitor was appointed to the Court of Queen's Bench, previously the sole domains of the trained barrister, to the great scandal of the Inns of Court. The barristers in Australia mounted a ferocious court challenge to solicitors encroaching on their previous exclusive territory, but they lost. When I was in Melbourne in 1993, I was shown a large television conference room by a leading solicitor, who proudly detailed the advocacy training that the younger solicitors in his firm were receiving from English barristers by closed circuit conferences.

I am certainly not distressed with the gradual abolition of the honorific Queens Counsel, because the recognition, purportedly by the Attorney General of the Province or the Attorney General of Canada, the Chief Law Officer of the Crown, of an individual as "One of Her Majesty's Counsel Learned in the Law" has become, certainly in my jurisdiction of Alberta, a desultory devalued honorific. I was appointed Queens Counsel in 1978, along with a classmate and trial lawyer colleague. We were the first of our law class to be so honoured. In those days one was honoured, because although there was sometimes a small rump of pals of government, the preferment of Queens Counsel still recognized that some barristers had earned the distinction of seniority and the right to wear the silk gown on their feet in the Courtroom. Queen's Counsel appointments were abolished in Ontario some years ago. In the result, a number of highly qualified barristers were not honored, and I can well understand that stuck in a few craws. Ontario has by far the largest Bar in Canada.

Some jurisdictions in Canada have maintained the honourific, others have abolished it.

Lawyers in my province apply to the provincial Attorney General to 'take silk'. Persons aspiring to the QC appointment in Alberta in recent years have actually set up campaign committees and inundated the incumbent Attorney General of the province with letters from colleagues and clients and others urging the appointment of the candidate. Some of the appointments in my Province have been questionable. It was not unusual for a Leader of the Bar to be dropped in favour of someone less qualified. Admission to the Inner Bar no longer has much meaning to the Profession. The only people who are still somewhat awed by the QC appointment are the public, and it is not fair to prospective clients needing representation by a Leader when one who has not earned the honour on his/her feet in the Courtroom touts his/her silk gown on the firm website.

In the first couple of decades of my practice, the suggestion that a barrister would actually 'apply' to be appointed Queen's Counsel was simply unheard of. Some of my contemporaries and I deplore the lamentable fact that among the aspirants to honourifics and awards and memberships are those who self-nominate and actively campaign for the gong or position, and importune one to "put a word in so-and-so's ear." My father had a saying: "A good wine needs no bush." Enough said.

Well, as they say, times change, and one has to adapt or perish, or, as in my case after fifty-one years, take down the shingle and take up single malt.

All the above said, and having shown all due deference to vigorous advocacy, always remember that the client is the enemy!

10

NOSTALGIE DE LA BAR

The decline and fall of the no-holds-barred Bar social function, and a farewell to camaraderie rate their own chapter. One emphasizes the camaraderie of the smaller Bar, and mourns its loss. There was a magical irreverence about the early Bar in my province, which manifested itself and came to the fore at the various well-attended Bar functions, for example, the Calgary Bar annual historical dinner, the QC dinner, the Judges' dinner, and others. It is hard to capture in words the collegiality and closeness of the practitioners in the early days of my profession.

I shall always remember the late criminal defence counsel Charlie Stewart's comment on a recent Bar dinner we had both attended. I observed that it had been a fine function. Charlie simply exclaimed: "The camaraderie!"

For nine consecutive years I emceed the Kosowan-Wachowich Game Dinner, probably the superlative Bench-Bar yearly social event ever. The dinner was sponsored by the Kosowan Wachowich law firm, but with a goodly number of Alberta lawyer hunters and fishermen donating game and fish which were cooked superbly by a Swedish chef who was likely kept in captivity and chained up in the basement. This was the finest example of the camaraderie of the profession that one could encounter. And there was no mercy shown to any 'personage'. The highlight of the evening would be 'the Toast to the Game', a daunting occasion of unmitigated ribaldry and opprobrium heaped upon the head of the unfortunate Leader of the Bar or Judge who thought that he or she had been honoured to give the toast.

One of my tasks as master of ceremonies was to introduce the head table. On one such occasion, I asked the Chief Justice of the Court of Queen's Bench and the Chief Judge of the Provincial Court of Alberta, his brother, to stand. I then advised the assembled audience: "I've been asked to comment on the mental acuity of the Chief Justice of the Court of Queen's Bench and the Chief Judge of the Provincial Court of Alberta. They could not pour piss out of a cowboy boot if the instructions were written on the heel."

In the 70s, the senior litigation partner at the prominent Fenerty firm, Bill McGillivray QC, was elevated to the position of Chief Justice of Alberta directly from the street, such was his reputation. The former Chief Justice and his colleagues on the provincial Appellate Court Bench were notably cold and forbidding, and as I have observed earlier, attempting to argue an appeal before them was like being a private in the Red Army on May Day saluting the remote trilby hats assembled on the roof of the Kremlin. Addressing the Calgary Bar at the dinner in his honour after his appointment as Chief Justice, Bill in the course of his speech said "I want the highest appellate court to be approachable, more human." There was an inexplicable dead silence in response to this very warm breakthrough. The Chief Justice squinted at his notes, then said, "I have in my notes in brackets the word 'Applause'…" Then the place broke up. In public speaking, timing is everything.

On another convivial occasion when I was fulfilling my duties as master of ceremonies, Chief Justice Val Milvain jumped up from his place at the head table and came to the podium where I was speaking and generously poured a large helping of red wine into my glass, which unfortunately at the time held a passable whisky. My reaction: "Thank you, Chief Justice, for ruining a perfectly good single malt with a toxic dose of cheap Algerian plonk!"

Interspersed with no-holds-barred Bar social functions one had the odd staid dinner, notably the Canadian Bar Association (Alberta branch) obligatory dinners for fashionable persons in the legal industry. At one of these I found myself seated uneasily with the then President of the Alberta Branch of the Canadian Bar and another Canadian Bar senior groupie, with mercifully the intervention of the Chief Justice of the Supreme Court Trial Division, Val Milvain. In the course of this dinner, the CBA (AB) President observed plonkingly that, to use his words, "In my capacity as President of the Alberta Branch of the Canadian Bar Association, I take great exception to some of your comments in your weekly column in the *Albertan* newspaper." In some columns, I had taken the mickey out of the local Bar, just for the fun of it. He dabbed his mouth with a napkin in disapproval of me. The riposte was offered by Milvain CJ: "I read all Evans' columns, and I know why he writes them." That was a grand vindication.

With the notable ascendancy of women in my profession, to which I have devoted one of the early chapters of this book, the Calgary Bar "Ladies Night" dinner soon became an anachronism. This was a yearly event, to which the members of the Profession – again, mostly male, there being so few female lawyers – brought their wives and girlfriends to a black tie dinner to be regaled with a soporific "toast to the ladies" from one of the Old Boys and a response to that toast by one of the senior Ladies. I still have nightmares recalling the year that the dinner speaker was Master in Chambers the Hon. Arthur Bessemer, since deceased, and as he declaimed upon "the beauty of Aphrodite as an example of female pulchitrude" – Jesus! – I remember taking my handkerchief and sticking an end in each ear. Amazement.

I attended only a few dinners in my declining years at the Bar, notably the Court of Appeal hundredth anniversary dinner, which was deadly. I have alluded to it earlier. Seven speakers preceded the honoured guest speaker, US Supreme Court Justice Antonin Scalia. Crammed in were some 750 to 800 lawyers and judges in dutiful attendance at the big Westin banquet room. I think the first course, the salad, came about 9:30 p.m.. By that time we had speeches up our fundament. It occurred to me that I did not know ninety percent of the lawyers there. More significantly, the ones I did know, particularly the gaggle of retired Court of Appeal justices who attended to preen and strut, and marvel at the dreadful videos of themselves that hit the audience from many screens, were people I did not want to see anyway.

I also went to the QC Dinner in 2016, mainly because my Firm associate Clayton Rice was appointed one of Her Majesty's Counsel, and he was more learned in the law than any other member of the head table. So he was worth it, but the event was terrible. I remember that out of the 700 or so lawyers who attended, most of them were deploying cellphones with frowning purpose, texting, watching some sports event. No one could hear the speeches, and the speakers were drowned out by constant talking throughout the crowd. This was outrageous. The only way to run these Bar social dinners is to have them hosted by no-nonsense types like some I could affectionately name from the old days, who shut up noise-makers and did not suffer fools and ran the proceedings with an iron hand.

Well, times change. Intimate Bar camaraderie was then and this is now, and in every Garden of Eden some acid rain must fall. The Bar is big and getting bigger. Calgary in the fifty years of my practice went from 300,000 or so to over 1,000,000. That's a sobering statistic.

The Alberta Legal Archives Society has an annual historical dinner. That is the only one that I am happy to attend, mainly because I know most of the old gang who go. They go mainly because they know most of the old gang who go.

The General Practitioner

In the 60s, and dying out in the 70s, one still encountered the general practitioner, that redoubtable fellow who drew a will one day and defended a careless driving charge the next day and sued on behalf of a small business client the day after that. Today we are so specialized that there are multiple sub-disciplines within disciplines, e.g., medical malpractice, drug defences, white-collar crime, Aboriginal law. At the solicitors' end, I expect there are all manner of enterprises labeled 'IPOs' and 'mergers and take-overs' that daily clog the business pages of the public prints and excite potential investors, the while enriching corporate lawyers beyond belief. The old general practitioner had no Persian rugs, no art on the walls, no expensive wallpaper in his dreary quarters in an office block that, however revered, had seen better days and was scheduled for the wrecker's ball, to be replaced by the Cosmo-Slotnick building. Or the Petro Canada building, known in my day and probably still today as 'Red Square', the legacy of the vile National Energy Program of then Prime Minister Pierre Elliott Trudeau.

When I was going to law school in Edmonton, in the summers I worked for my Stepfather Ross Campbell's insurance agency. One time he sent me around to the decayed chambers of a grizzled general practitioner to deliver some policy or other. I attended before this gentleman, who looked at whatever it was I had to deliver, and pronounced sniffishly "Campbell knows as much about insurance as Pete knows about muskets." I had no idea what Pete knew about muskets, but I duly reported this to my Stepfather, who was greatly amused. I say at once that the general practitioner was invariably a male person. Remember that when I started practicing law in 1963, there were only seven women admitted to law practice in the Province of Alberta.

The Benchers' Hind-Quarterly

The Canadian Bar Association (Alberta branch) and the Law Society of Alberta put out a joint newsletter that most of us called The Benchers' Hind-Quarterly, full of advertisements for themselves. My friend John Martland QC – the "M" – became the President of the Law Society. It was obligatory for this organ to publish a front page story on the new president, but Martland declined, "unless C.D. Evans writes the piece." Well, we had great fun. I spent a bit of time on The Wild Colonial Boys, Martland's very successful folk group that continued to do gigs for some forty years. Along the way, we made a ribald sport of the law and lawyers and lawyer governance.

We were now into the late 1980s, and tolerances at the Bar had changed. The Journal received letters condemning our bad taste and our lapse into humour. One such missive decried making fun of our profession, and was signed at the end or foot thereof with the pompous sobriquet 'corporate counsel'! My response to this pathetic plaint was that this old world, especially the legal world, could use some laughter. The M and I kept laughing in any event. We found this tremendously humorous, of course, and still do.

The Bar Admission Course, then and now

The only law school in Alberta up to the seventies was the University of Alberta Faculty of Law, which produced generations of Alberta judges and lawyers. Anyone from anywhere else was looked upon with deep suspicion.

My articling year was relatively stress-free. In contrast to today's regime of lectures, papers, apprenticeship in criminal, civil, divorce and solicitors chambers, and the daunting entrance exam, my contemporaries in 1963 gathered about once a month at the Courthouse so that we could be regaled by a 'senior practitioner' with his Life and Times. The Exam consisted of fifty questions to be answered true or false. Luckily, my year was 'false', and I got fifty-two percent or something, and was Admitted to the Bar on Friday, November 13, 1964. That's how I became a lawyer. Years later, I found myself as one of the lecturers at the Bar Admission courses beefed up by the Law Society that were mandatory for articled students. Our curriculum was devised by my former boss and great friend Paul Chrumka QC, later Mr. Justice Chrumka of the Alberta Court of Queen's Bench, and he set the exam. I admitted to him that, even after some 15 years in the practice of criminal law, I could not pass it.

"Not a member of The Club"

A standing criticism leveled at this or that poor wretch in those days was that he was "not a member of the club." I say 'he' because in those early days no women were permitted membership in any prominent private social clubs in Calgary. When I was inexplicably elected a Bencher of the Law Society in late 1977, I received a phone call from a Bar leader who was the incoming president of the Law Society: "Welcome to the club!" Oh dear.

In the early days of my practice, practically every 'successful' lawyer was a member of the Ranchmen's Club on 13th Avenue SW, housed then as now in a delightfully charming but somewhat dated edifice. It has since been renovated inside and outside. A number of its members were also decayed edifices. The place was exclusively male for decades. Members' wives were obliged to use the rear entrance and were not entitled to enter the elaborate front doors. Stuffed animal heads adorned the walls, and there was the obligatory panel of stuffed heads of Past Presidents. Speaking of the remote row of trilby hats, a smoking room on the ground floor, replete with leather chairs and the pearl push button to imperiously summon a waiter, was known as the Kremlin. The Kremlin was exclusively the domain of members of the Alberta Court of Appeal, and no one dared enter without their specific invitation. There the Old Boys sat around smoking cigars and quaffing single malt and commenting adversely on the Decline of the Profession.

The Calgary Golf and Country Club membership was also obligatory even if one did not commit the offense of golf.

On the passing of a Member, there would always be the social gathering subsequent to the planting at the Ranchmen's or the Golf and Country Club, dreary affairs washed down with lashings of whisky.

One recalls the old Chamber of Commerce building, downtown, and the entrance to the Chamber Club. In my novel "The Pox Doc's Clerk," the villainous Dr. Sleeth meets the fraudulent Dr. Fallopius for lunch at what sounds like the Chamber Club. As we are looking back in time, it is worth noting up. This venue required mid to top-level management or civil service positions as eligibility for the perquisites of membership. A wall of photographs exhibited a display of one ear, one nose former Presidents of the Chamber, arranged in chronological order starting with a faded photo of some latter 19th century twit with staring eyes in a pudding face mounted in a celluloid collar and framed with a plug hat. Above the portraits was a ramshackle collection of assorted group photos taken on miscellaneous occasions of civic self-congratulation. Most of those depicted, of course men, would pose with both hands fastened to their coat lapels; all wore ferocious expressions, ferocious mustaches and outrageous hats. There were no women in the photographs. Cattle barons, whiskey traders, operators of establishments of ill fame. It was possible in those days to belong to all three groups.

Speaking of clubs, not many criminal lawyers belong to Rotary, but it is enthusiastically attended by the corporate legal crowd. "God was the first Rotarian!" was a great line commencing the speech of a notable Rotarian, duly noted by H.L. Menken in his collection Americana, having found it in a 1929 American newspaper reporting a Rotary event. I had occasion to make the following observation in my newspaper column circa 1975: "When a policeman comes to my front door, I am, like any citizen, afraid, but I open the door. When a Rotarian comes to my front door, I run out the back door." Some years later, absurd as it may sound, I was contacted by a perfervid fellow who was apparently retained to write a glowing history of Rotary in Calgary. His telephone message was to the effect that he had read the above comment, was disturbed by it, and wanted to interview me on why I was hostile to Rotary. Needless to say, I did not return the call. But I had a good cackle.

The only club I ever 'belonged to' for my entire practice was the YMCA Health Club, also known as the Club Foot, because it had a steam room and the general locker room did not. Last year, I succumbed to unbridled comfort and joined the Ranchmen's Club, sponsored by two valued colleagues. There I dine on occasion in solitary splendor in the dining room known as the Wolves Den.

All Calgary private clubs today have many women and all races as members. That, if you remember the old days, could be said to be revolutionary.

Law Firm "Branding"

Noting that a substantial Calgary law firm had 'amalgamated' with a similar British legal firm, I revisited the revolutionary development of national and then international law firms. I suppose they are not a bad thing, as they improve the competition for legal services in the places where they open branch offices, but it must be tough hewing to be one of 1,300 or so partners and to argue with some obscure points committee on the allotted quantum of one's annual stipend – dependent upon one's "billings" and attraction of new clients – while attending the annual partners' meeting in some fancy resort or other. Most of these outfits, and indeed some of the local large firms, are now obsessed with what they call 'branding'. They adopt an acronym or name or even a logo of some sort that identifies them at large, and appoint 'marketing directors' and 'entertainment coordinators'!

It is not much of a leap to decry Law Firm 'branding' and the wholesale restructuring of legal firms to global marketing as a far cry from, and a churlish repudiation of, the noble Profession of Thomas Erskine KC, Sir Edward Carson QC, Edward Marshall Hall QC, Chief Justice Valentine Milvain and their inspiring like.

I have always said that the strength of this Profession is not found in the great sonorously omnipotent legal mills with their Persian rugs and overpriced artwork, but is found in every young lawyer who gets on her or his hind legs in a hostile courtroom before an incompetent or stupid judge, opposed by a sanctimonious puke of a prosecutor, defending a notoriously opprobrious client who has lied and prevaricated from day one, and says, in a calm and confident and clear voice, "I defend this prisoner!"

The suggestion that a law firm, purporting to be made up of professionals who have qualified to practice our Profession, should be obsessed with the efficacy of its 'brand' at large is anathema to those of us who are practicing Barristers.

In closing, one could well ask, what is to regret with the passing of those early years? Nostalgia is a powerful emotional sentiment that infects all of us at a certain age and perspective, when we find ourselves making comparisons and noting contrasts. Conclusion: one is at one with the moneyed old bag in *Beyond the Fringe's* superb satire on The War: "I said to my husband – as he then was – Squiffy, this is the end of an era."

11

OTHER INNOVATIONS

"Revolutions always attract the wrong sorts of people", observed Alan Bennett, the prominent British writer. Robert Fulford, Canadian philosopher emeritus, noted that "widespread talk of revolution sometimes produces hucksters who wonder what's in it for them."

Philip Larkin in a letter to novelist Barbara Pym, July 1969 observed: "It was a disagreeable experience. I suppose revolutions always are."

With revolutions, the long-established entrenched plutocracy or oligarchy gives way to reformists, they evolve into or are replaced by radicals, they in turn are replaced by lunatics, until the pendulum swings back, and enter a dictator or even a liberal democracy seizing power at the flood. Along the way, the radicals turn on the moderate reformers and throw them out, then the extremists turn on the radicals, then the extremists turning lunatics turn on themselves. Nature abhors a vacuum: hail, Napoleon Bonaparte! Full circle.

The reader will conclude that I have concluded that not all of the revolutionary events of the last 50 years have been positive. But other innovations I am ambivalent about. I deal with them in this chapter.

Victims

Victimhood gone rampant is a relatively recent development in the legal arena. In the past, embracing the first two decades of my practice, apparent victims – unless the *corpus delicti* – were either sorrowful members of the courtroom audience or witnesses with no special status beyond apparently having some personal knowledge of the matters in issue in the criminal litigation which affected them negatively. As such, in either camp, they were not given any special treatment or distinction. Of course, one fully appreciated that for just about every crime there was an alleged victim or victims, which rather points up the oft-cited mitigating factor of an accused having committed a crime "without a victim", for example, trafficking in marijuana. (I observe that 'victimless crimes' are the work product of the grim-faced puritan, whom H.L. Mencken properly condemned as "One who has the horrible feeling that someone, somewhere, might be having a good time.")

It gradually dawned upon the proletarian consciousness in around the 1970s that there was virtue in victimhood; it was a badge of distinction to be sought after.

In the course of my practice, police administrations and other public agencies routinely appointed social workers to provide 'victims' assistance', which included counselling, encouragement to proceed with the allegation, and accompaniment to court and sitting with the 'victim' in the witness room. The victim business really got serious in the case of alleged victims of sexual assault: hand-holding and sympathy and the cultivation of vengeance upon the wretched accused, be he ever so innocent, from the very hour of the complaint through to and including the exhaustion of all appeals. Where the complainant is a child of tender years, the victim's assistant is often a combination of both the investigating police officer, said to be particularly trained to investigate children's complaints sympathetically, together with a kind social worker type who is designated not only to befriend and accompany the child before, during, and after criminal proceedings, but to actually sit with the child in the witness box or in the room where she or he is testifying by television so she/he does not have to be in the presence of the accused.

Participating in a panel on sexual assault in Vancouver, I was asked by the chairperson how I defended a child molester. My response:

"I put my head down on the counsel table and cry!"

These innovations have been deemed by investigating authorities and victims' support groups and prosecutors to be necessary, but they have turned the presumption of innocence on its head: in some cases, it is now the presumption of guilt. A certain species of Crown counsel abandoned the time-honoured dictum of Mr. Justice Rand to conduct themselves as 'ministers of justice' and perfervidly embraced the role of victim's advocate. This is the prosecutorial social worker mentality that deliberately refers to the complainant in a criminal case before a jury as 'the victim', and the accused as 'the prisoner'.

Another legislative sop to victimhood is the 'victim impact statement' mandated by the *Criminal Code*, whereby, for the purpose of determining the sentence to be imposed on some poor wretch, "the court shall consider any statement that may have been prepared... of a victim of the offence describing the harm done to, or loss suffered by, the victim arising from the commission of the offence." The statement, prepared in writing and filed with the court, on the request of the victim may be read by the victim. It may include "any other evidence concerning any victim of the offence for the purpose of determining the sentence to be imposed," which can embrace irrelevant or vindictive minutiae. 'Victim' includes "any person to whom harm was done or who suffered physical or emotional loss as a result of the commission of the offence," which covers just about any relative or friend of the real victim. Of course, the real victim may be dead, but if dead, ill or otherwise incapacitated, the spouse or common-law partner or "any relative of that person" or anyone with some sort of connection can get up and bemoan.

To have to sit through the reading of these things is cruel and unusual punishment. They are not very helpful to a court of competent criminal jurisdiction where it is presumed that victims have greatly suffered and the court always recognizes this fact.

The excellent Christie Blatchford, nationally syndicated columnist specializing in the criminal justice system, made some telling comments in the *National Post* edition of Saturday, April 27, 2013, entitled 'How much deference for victims?' She attended a 'disposition hearing' of a person found not criminally responsible in the violent death of a police officer. A total of six victim impact statements were read: by the widow; by relatives of the deceased; and by a colleague.

Ms. Blatchford noted compassionately that it was obvious that those good people who had lost an exemplary citizen were in great pain. She notes also that there were suggestions that the justice system had let them down because the family would have to endure the review process, and that the accused would never be forgiven.

As one who has witnessed and reported upon many significant court proceedings, Ms. Blatchford states that victim impact statements are meant to have a limited use: they are "one of many factors a judge considers in determining sentence." She says they are not meant to be either a tribute to the victim or a chance to beat up on an offender.

With which perceptive observations I agree.

Provincial and federal 'human rights legislation' courts might well be temples for the exaltation of victimhood. I have made observations of these tribunals – some of them positive – in their own section in this chapter.

All that said, here I shall say a word for the genuine victim who has suffered mightily and is heavily put upon. Alberta established the Crimes Compensation Board, before whom a victim of a crime who suffered actual damages – e.g. injuries, property damage, loss of income – could apply for some modest compensation. With its limited mandate, it was and remains a good idea.

I did have one experience attending as counsel for an applicant before the Alberta Crimes Compensation Board. My client was very much a pitiable victim: it was the most sordid fact situation wherein the convicted accused had kidnapped this rather diminutive, retiring person and committed the most brutal and invasive assault imaginable. Quite rightly, this poor fellow was taken by me before the Board, the actual pecuniary loss which would be the maximum of his entitlement not being one iota comparable to his physical and mental suffering. The Board at that time was Chaired by a courteous and gentle barrister. I also recall the two other appointees to the three-person board were typical examples of semi-retired citizens who presumably had at some point some connection with the provincial government. One of these was a particularly abrasive pomposity with whom I got into an argument. But for the intervention of the evenhanded Chairman, I'm sure I would have left the Counsel table and taken this fellow by the throat. I thought, if that was the way some commissioners treated a senior counsel, how did they treat some poor wretch who staggered in without a lawyer!

Human Rights Tribunals

Another 'revolution' in the legal profession was the proliferation in Canada of 'human rights' tribunals, alarmingly criticized by their detractors as a sort-of a spinoff of excess and misdirected revolutionary zeal akin to the Committee of Public Safety, Paris, circa 1793. To their critics, a human rights tribunal 'hearing' is the equivalent of the Soviet era 'show trial', and their trenchant criticisms of human rights tribunals have been vociferous. They are criticized as products of a polity that has been subjected to overarching 'political correctness' and the stifling of freedom of expression.

I have not had personal experience before these boards. I confess, influenced by the negative propaganda, that I had harbored a bad impression of these human rights tribunals. It appeared to critics that rather than providing a necessary forum for abused or badly used citizens with genuine grievances, they were providing sounding boards for some of the nutters that afflict the general population. Critics charged that anyone with 'hurt feelings', who had no cause of action in a civil court – that might be contemplated and redressed by Courts of law, after hearing evidence and weighing credibility – could get in front of a human rights tribunal and could make some sort of absurd complaint or other against an employer or a neighbor, and get away with it but allegedly be spared the expense of hiring a lawyer or paying costs of the other side.

I viewed them with scepticism, however, my information critical of them was hearsay and third hand. The principal criticisms of human rights tribunals portrayed by their detractors have been broadcast at large and include: the provision at taxpayers' expense of a public forum for the airing of grievances against individuals or entities that raise no cause of action eligible to be tried in a court of law; that some of their functionaries are allegedly overzealous; the presiding Boards are not apparently governed by any rules of evidence and can allow hearsay and lay person opinion into evidence and receive testimony that a lawyer might consider is neither credible nor probative; that they can award financial compensation to a complainant who would not have any prospect of establishing a case in a court of law; in the event that a complaint is dismissed as unfounded, the complainant, who has been granted all the advantages of investigation and advice without putting up one cent, has not had to pay any legal fees nor is he or she assessed costs, and the respondent is stuck with both, having to use his or her own resources to retain counsel.

These allegations, if made out, are good reasons not to be enthusiastic about such tribunals that popped up both federally and in most provinces. But one reasonably expects that human rights tribunals as well as courts and other public forums can from time to time be abused by bogus litigants and complainants. That is the way of the world.

It appears to me that human rights tribunals provide a necessary forum for the citing of genuine grievances, say, against a nasty landlord or a hateful neighbor or a harassing or discriminating employer, delicts that would not attain the status of a 'cause of action' in a court of law, but which should be heard and, if appropriate, redressed by an adjudicative body. A lot of gentle people get pushed around by cads and bullies, and cannot afford today's legal fees. Genuinely aggrieved, they consult a lawyer and get a huge bill with the advice that they have 'no claim in law'. So they have recourse to a human rights tribunal, and sometimes a sympathetic ear. What is adverse about that, in today's society that counsels inclusiveness and diversity, and abhors discrimination, racism, bigotry, and bullying?

I have perused the *Alberta Human Rights Act*, and I do not find its provisions to be startling. It commences with the preamble that all persons are equal in dignity and that 'multiculturalism describes the diverse racial and cultural composition of Alberta society', and there is a 'diverse racial and cultural composition of society' that we are all aware of and appreciate. Particular sections deal with discrimination in services, facilities, tenancy, employment practices, prohibiting discrimination against any person 'because of race, religious beliefs, gender... physical disability, mental disability, ancestry, place of origin' and so on.

The *Act* says that no person shall retaliate against a person who has made a complaint under the Act, but no person shall make a complaint that is frivolous or vexatious, with malicious intent. The contravention complaint must be shown to have been 'reasonable and justifiable in the circumstances.'

Investigators are appointed; they have certain powers. If the matter cannot be resolved, a human rights tribunal is appointed to deal with the complaint. Parties may be represented by counsel. Of note, "Evidence may be given before a human rights tribunal in any manner that the tribunal considers appropriate, and the tribunal is not bound by the rules of law respecting evidence in judicial proceedings." The tribunal, if it finds the complaint without merit, may dismiss it; if it finds a complaint has merit, may make an order against the respondent to cease and refrain from the contravention, to compensate the person for loss of wages or income or expenses incurred, and "may make any order as to costs that it considers appropriate." It is noteworthy that the Alberta tribunal has an open power to award costs, and presumably in a proper case could order costs against a complainant where the complaint was patently specious and frivolous.

More recent developments in Alberta have also given me pause. The current Chair of the Alberta Human Rights Commission is a highly respected retired Queen's Bench Justice before whom I appeared many times in court, and whom I also opposed from time to time when he was at the Bar. One of his contemporaries, who in fact was my old boss when I was a prosecutor, and who is one of the most esteemed and competent judges who ever sat on the High Court in this province, now also retired from the Court, is currently presiding at tribunal hearings. I cannot imagine either of these principled jurists departing from the necessity to abide by some rules of evidence, the reasoned assessment of credibility, and a mature and professional characterization and appropriate resolution of the issue.

Intervenors

The early years of my court practice, criminal and civil, featured the representation of the Crown or the defence, or either a plaintiff or defendant, on occasion a 'third-party' brought in by the defendant's motion to pay the freight if things went against the defence. That is, litigation was between party and party, and outsiders were not welcome. 'Intervenors' were a new phenomenon to have to contend with, often deluging one with tons of paper: a person or more often an organization, like an NGO, with high sounding principles and a big budget who applied to the court to present a brief and, if permitted, argument on an issue presumably of national interest incidentally raised by the civil proceeding or criminal case.

This sort of intervention was anathema to many of us, particularly in hard fought criminal cases where the only issue of interest to the Crown or the defence was that of credibility of witnesses. We resented a party and party contest being hijacked by some outfit that we alleged trespassed upon a private dispute. One could argue one's client's case through various levels of court only to find that the ultimate decision might turn on an issue that someone else, who was not a party, had raised. I complained of this publicly, often to the great amusement of assorted judiciary, many of whom were pleased to have the court assisted by outside agencies on significant issues, example, sexual assault. Intervening organizations turned up in all sorts of cases, with volunteer counsel presenting voluminous briefs and arguments to appellate courts and the Supreme Court of Canada. My former law firm associate and friend Dr. the Hon. Justice Sheilah Martin of the Alberta Court of Appeal argued notable interventions for the Women's Legal Education and Action Fund – LEAF – in the Supreme Court of Canada. LEAF is a national organization "that exists to ensure the equality rights of women and girls under the law," grounded in section 15 of the *Charter*. LEAF performs legal research and intervenes in appellate and Supreme Court of Canada cases on women's issues; it has intervened in many significant sittings of the Supreme Court. Justice Martin has been a major innovator and advocate of interventions, and would certainly not endorse my lukewarm comments.

Here I am obliged to own up that I indeed made an application to intervene in an existing civil litigation. It was the late 90s, and some lunatic had been suing Crown attorneys. In fact, he was suing just about everybody, until the Chief Justice of the day made an order prohibiting him from commencing a lawsuit by filing a statement of claim. Along the way, he sued the Alberta Crown attorneys for something or other. They were very ably defended by leading counsel of the Civil Section of the Attorney General's Department. The aggravating litigator was defeated at trial, and appealed. The Crown Attorneys Association approached me to apply for standing at the Appellate level to argue on their behalf. I made an application before a three-person court chaired by the Hon. Mr. Justice Stratton. Joe Stratton frowned a lot when I got up to make my application. He asked me: "What can you add to what counsel for the Attorney General will submit?" I replied, "The pleasure of my company." That caused the other two members of the Court to have a cackle, but Justice Stratton was having none of it, and my application was dismissed. The Crown Attorneys insisted that I send them a bill, and I insisted that I would not. My learned friend David Doherty QC, subsequently on the Ontario Court of Appeal, had made a similar application for the Ontario Crown Attorneys a couple of years back, declined to send them a bill, and was presented with a very handsome briefcase. A month or so after my Court of Appeal application, the President of the Alberta Crown Attorneys Association arrived in my chambers with a beautiful pigskin briefcase as a gift from his members. I still carry it every day, even though briefcases appear to have been supplanted or replaced by shoulder harnesses for soft bags that contain computers and other stuff for the modern executive. In late 2013, I was lined up at the Kelowna airport, and a man behind me said, touching my briefcase, "You know that's an antique." Some antiques one treasures.

I have to observe the more positive note on interveners was struck for me in the *Krieger* case, which I have spoken about in this book. By the time I got to the Supreme Court of Canada there were seven or eight Intervenors on each side, Federal Justice and some provincial Attorneys General and Crown prosecutors associations on my side, and Law Societies and criminal defence associations on the other side. It was kind of comforting to go into the highest Court with a contingent of like-minded advocates in support. We lost, by the way, nine zip.

The Legalization of Drugs

As for the legalization of the dread cannabis, I am all for it. Not so much for blow, but one might as well tax the hell out of users.

I reasonably expect that continued medical and pharmacological research will establish that marijuana is more beneficial than harmful. Of course, there is always the lunatic fringe who become 'addicted' – psychologically, in any event – to the weed. The worst that they appear to get up to is to sit around smoking dope and doing nothing else. Exactly what the large proportion of the population is doing in front of its TV sets. I have yet to hear of any driver of a motor vehicle committing any mayhem or running anybody down having had a joint. Marijuana's therapeutic medical properties have not been exaggerated by the qualified members of the medical profession who prescribe it to patients. One balks at the outrageous hypocrisy of liquor and beer drinkers over centuries of abuse of their lethal and bodily destructive vice of choice in condemning the dread cannabis, and in slinging any person caught in simple possession into the common gaol and leaving them with a criminal record.

The announced intent of the Federal government of the day at this writing is that new legislation will make the sale of marijuana in Canada legal by July 1, 2018. Marijuana should be legal and able to be procured at a reasonable price at government controlled retail outlets, the government effectively controlling cultivation and distribution and doing away with any profit factor in private trafficking, emulating some US states. Provinces will have the right to decide how marijuana is distributed and sold.

Obviously, law authorities will have to wrestle with proof to the requisite standard that a motor vehicle or boat driver was operating the vehicle while 'impaired' by the ingestion of marijuana.

Cocaine, *dubitante*: if any citizen insists on enhancing his/her congenital incompetence by shoving toxic white powder up their proboscis, that person is badly wanted out of the workforce and down and out on the streets. Those who blow their ill-gotten gains on 'blow' i.e. on cocaine, are welcome to do so as long as they don't annoy or interfere with the rest of us. Inevitably, societal shunning will exert its expected rebuke.

All things considered, snorting cocaine through a rolled-up bill cannot be as deleterious to one's Jack Ripper 'vital bodily fluids' as inhaling a Monte Cristo or Romeo and Juliet while mainlining a prodigious quantity of single malt, a.k.a. lighter fluid. No one criticizes the cigar smoker, an aficionado of William Claude Dukenfield's classic iconic line: "A woman is just a woman, but a good cigar is a smoke!" If cigarettes and whiskey – vices that are universally accepted and heavily taxed – and wild wild women drive you crazy, drive you insane, cocaine is ideal for the less adventurous. Best if the government gets in the business of purchasing the product and selling it to the public at a price that undercuts the traffickers.

Meanwhile, back on society's mean streets, the locus of the War on Drugs – such as debilitating and killing drugs like heroin and opium derivatives – that War, that costs the taxpayers so much, is already lost. Irredeemable addicts of the killer drugs are useless to and a drain upon society, but they have to be cared for by the rest of us. Users enrich the traffickers, and the sordid trade prospers. That war has to continue; there is no option with killer drugs.

As to cocaine, there is an option. In Columbia, production of coca, the raw material for cocaine, has reached record levels. *The Economist* reports that the President of Bolivia recently signed a law to expand the area on which the cultivation of coca is allowed. That weekly comprehensive newspaper reports that the President is a former leader of the coca-growers union, and he defends the crop "as a traditional stimulant." Demand in North America for the 'traditional stimulant' is high and apparently on the rise. There is something like a sixty percent increase in the number of young persons who admitted to trying it for the first time. Powerful drug cartels smuggle it into the US, deploying hidden compartments in vehicles, high-powered speedboats, or shoved up human mules. Overdose deaths involving cocaine occur; overdose deaths from alcohol also occur. The bottom line is that cocaine is not going away, and the government might as well get in on it and use the money for roads, infrastructure, schools and hospitals.

That solution, of course, is the obvious one that has been floating around – in some places, barely afloat – for a couple of decades now, but the debate has been re-vitalized by the decision in Canada and some US jurisdictions to legalize marijuana: legalize as well some illicit drugs, e.g. cocaine, with the government, as with dope, going into the import business and the marketing business for incredible profits that can build hospitals and schools and restore decaying infrastructure, ameliorate the neglected Armed Forces, and be shoveled into anti-drug abuse education initiatives.

I fully realize that expressing these views so forcefully will hardly commend me to the further tolerance of my criminal law practice colleagues, many of whom earn generous livings defending persons accused of what we call 'drug offences'.

But they have no cause to be troubled by these observations: the possibility of the government of the day to consider any legislation even approaching the legalization of drugs like cocaine or the commercial advantages occasioned thereby, not to mention the steep decline in the crime rate, is so remote as to be laughable, mainly because it is so sensible and forward thinking.

12

FINAL WORDS

I commence this final chapter of my book with the observation that the Age of Enlightenment has been supplanted by the Age of Entitlement. Witness today's self-esteem culture: Every child who participates in school soccer matches gets a trophy. "Today is all about ourselves!" "Celebrate ourselves," and so on.

'Affirmative action', that is, programs and initiatives benefitting the competent disadvantaged and disabled and the racially discriminated, is positive; it might even be said to be 'revolutionary'. But subsidizing the botched who normally would fail is not.

One of the first pleasurable tasks I set myself on first going on the inactive list was to finish a play in which the protagonist, who was obliged to suffer a stale-dated prosecution for sexual assault, is represented by an incompetent defence counsel who stutters so badly that he cannot ask a question in cross-examination, the Crown is represented by a perfervid individual who suffers from obsessive compulsions, and the judge has Tourette syndrome and is constantly screaming obscenities. Of course, they held their offices due to affirmative action. No local production company would touch it. QED.

I have always firmly subscribed to the view that this harsh old world, and in particular the structured and strictured world of The Law, needs the tonic of laughter. "Plant the seeds of laughter," the great Calgary barrister and raconteur Paddy Nolan said, almost one hundred years ago, so I am not alone. In his Editor's note to Hunter

S. Thompson's *Fear and Loathing in America*, Douglas Brinkley stated "…. against the assault of laughter nothing can stand, at least not for long." I find myself too frequently bemused by the po-faced if 'sincere' lugubriosities of my colleagues of the Bench and Bar, not to mention the absurdities emanating at large from the general population.

One of the great traditions in the English background which I inherited in my genes and have benefited from, and another reason why the British are inimitable, is the admirable penchant for Englishmen to take the piss out of pomposities and/or overblown events. The pompous if hapless persons targeted may be well-meaning and even sincere, always recalling George Bernard Shaw's putdown of 'sincerity': "It is dangerous to be sincere, unless you are also stupid."

Using the term 'taking the piss' with almost any North American, even clerisy, invites a query as to what exactly one means. There are variants, the most common the traditional Irish 'Taking the Mickey'. Joyful example: the editors of *Private Eye* magazine targeting the English Court of Appeal as dumb cows on their cover, then standing trial in the prisoners' dock of The Old Bailey for Scandalizing the Court, attired in gym slips and fright wigs brandishing field hockey sticks. They were defended by the redoubtable English QC and author John Mortimer.

On many occasions I have, with great hilarity, taken the mickey out of colleagues and judges. In most of the cases, affronted - and not getting the great good humour of it – the targets did not reply. Harrumph! Patrick O'Brian in Post Captain: "….but there are not many who can find themselves the object of open, whole-hearted, sincere, protracting laughter without being put out of countenance…"

Genuine laughter is now in short supply among lawyers; frantic inoffensiveness is the career wise posture. Today's majority have had their better instincts and their sensibilities constantly propagandized, blunted, and tailored to the times by the same humourless social engineers and moral uplifters and goose-steppers who work the machine in Kafka's *In The Penal Colony*. Lawyers, even the more broad-minded Criminal Bar, have wholeheartedly embraced the repressive and stultifying precepts of the School of Political Correctness, an overworked phrase and concept I would abjure if it were not so apposite. A dead hand has fallen upon impudence, doubt, and dissent, the very rationales for our Profession in the first place. 'Taking the Mickey' is punishable by Coventry. For some of us, obviously, it was time to go. We had not made it through evolution, into the Law Society's second century. We disturbed the New Order. The consensus is that it is as well for the Profession that the likes of me has been relegated, stuffed with my own barrister's wig, to the Royal Tyrrell Museum of Paleontology.

In the Law Society book I confessed that I belonged more to that old mercenary school that never confused defending criminals with social work. This is a free and voluntary confession, not made under torture, and in accordance with the hallowed strictures of *Ibrahim v. The King.* In my somewhat jaundiced world, and that of the ancient Alberta Criminal Bar, it took my client four years to steal the money, it took me four weeks to get it from him, he went to jail, I did not. Ergo, the system worked.

"Well," one laments, "it's not the way things used to be...." But that was then; this is now. I think the contrast is that, with most of my contemporaries, we had knocked around a bit before taking up the law. For example, my current law firm associate, a ten year RCMP officer with five kids, enforcing the law before he went to the law. It was not – got born, went to school, went to university, went to law school, became a criminal lawyer. To some extent at least, my generation had sampled what Edmund Burke termed "the rich, ripe fruit of experience".

Having got all that self-congratulation for higher sensibility and worldliness off my chest, I also have to note that it is almost axiomatic and customary for old lawyers to indulge in a lot of unfair criticism of young lawyers. The usual multiple harangue is along the following lines: many of them have appalling manners, no social graces whatsoever, totally self absorbed and suffused with the need to maintain their "self-esteem", fat-headed, rapacious, absurdly combative, functionally illiterate, historically and encyclopaedically ignorant, demonstrating no interest in the creative process, no sense of wonder.

This typical diatribe purports to illuminate an alleged contrast between old barristers and today's young lawyers. It is more accurately the ranting hackneyed observations of old men about the younger generation, that is, "All going to hell in a handbasket!" Somehow the new generation will muddle through, and old farts like me appropriately consigned to the scrap heap. But what I sensed in 2005 when I said "I did not leave my profession, my profession left me" may be accurate.

Writing a memoir that is also a legal history, one of course wishes to be inclusive, but as with *A Painful Duty*, many of my drafts have been condemned to the cutting room floor because there is simply not space to write about every interesting colleague or occurrence in a long career. As a bad example, my collection of anecdotes commenting adversely on some "learned friends" who were not so learned and not so friendly. For a positive example, the Hon. Russell Dixon, retired Justice of the Court of Queen's Bench, on or about his 92nd birthday – having just finished a game of tennis – sent me his own memoirs of a career on the Bench preceded by his years in practice following overseas service as a paratrooper in the Second World War, poignantly including photos and observations from the point of view of an eighteen year old soldier. Fascinating stuff, and reminiscent of Colin Gunner's memoir *Adventures with the Irish Brigade* that he sent to Philip Larkin.

Larkin noted to Gunner, October 1971:

> It does seem an original book, in that it's a war narrative by someone who actually seems to enjoy remembering it, even if he didn't at the time, and thinks it did him good, or at least was worth doing.

Regrettably, I am not able to include Russ's lively articles and observations in this memoir, anymore than I can resurrect my previous draft chapter detailing letters over years from highly literate friends, 'Men and Women of Letters'. There is just no room, and this memoir is dealing with a revolution in my Profession, so those pieces will have to be for another day.

The only other colleague I know of who keeps a commonplace book is Richard Peck QC of Vancouver. Not only do we exchange books, but we also exchange our journal entries. A commonplace book is to be distinguished from a daily journal: one does not necessarily make an entry on a daily basis, and also not necessarily to record the events of one's life, as opposed to recording the thoughts of others that are worthy of repetition. Some daily thoughts of others are worth reading.

• • •

I feel obliged to comment on the Post-truth Era:

Speaking of 'reflections', Rick Peck QC gifted me Arthur Koestler's engaging *Reflections on Hanging*. I gave Richard my US first edition of Orwell's *1984*. *1984* regained new prominence – and an emergency 75,000 volume re-printing – on the election and inauguration of US President Donald Trump in January 2017. A matter of interest is one columnist's discussion of 1984, wherein he advised reading Koestler's *Darkness at Noon* first. All this brings into focus nationalistic xenophobia in the world's Western liberal democracies, and a concurrent popular surge to isolation, protectionism, and anti-globalization in what writers and thinkers are calling 'the post-truth era'.

As to objective truth, it appears a large number of voters in most Western democracies simply do not like immigrants because they dislike hearing foreign languages emanating from people who look different, they mistrust cultures other than their own, and they assume all foreigners are trouble. A lot of these voters are not bad people, simply ignorant and simple minded. They complain that 'the system' is not working for them, that all sorts of criminals and terrorists are coming across relaxed borders, that AI automation and immigrants are doing them out of jobs and affordable housing and the newcomers are getting generous welfare and being supported by taxpayers' money.

Objective truth – basic facts, which are not relative things whose refutation is presented as 'alternative facts' – today may well be 'crimethink'. Post-truth is doublespeak, presented under the guise of 'alternative facts'. That is right out of Orwell! In the post-truth era, there is a rejection of expertise and intellectualism by the majority of populations, and the passive acceptance of outright lies and nonsense foisted on them by some political leaders.

And it does not help matters to learn that 2015 World Book Day research indicates one in ten people do not own a single book, and among eighteen to twenty-four-year-olds, that number rises to one in five!

At the writing of this book, we are living through truly revolutionary times in world affairs: witness the traumatic shock waves of Brexit, Trump, the second French Revolution; and the rising tide in 'western' countries of brutal acts of terrorism. In Canada, it appears that if one has the temerity to make allowance for legitimate criticism of Islamic terror, and allowance for legitimate criticism of Islam (or of any religion), one is accused of 'Islamophobia' and stands condemned by all right-thinking persons. The nationally renowned writer Rex Murphy observed: "… the great swath of the Canadian public… are not reflexively or otherwise 'haters of Islam' and are appalled by the very notion." I concur.

Meanwhile, not many voices speak out against the sinister spread of anti-Semitism. Overseas, a shifting European Union is rebelling against an entrenched, dictatorial Euro bureaucracy (the tumbrels will roll again); there is weakened NATO alertness; countries and people seem to tolerate an assertive bullying Russian Federation in Europe and the Middle East. Rogue states menace all of us. North Korea, which is run by a violent dictator, is advancing in developing a ballistic missile with sufficient range to deliver a nuclear warhead to the US continent. Further, it was openly and defiantly offering the technology it had developed on the global market, allegedly disclosing destabilizing nuclear material to other rogue and outlaw states around the world. Iran is the principal supporter of terrorist cadres in the world, its people subjected and cowed by its wacko all-powerful religious leaders and the so-called Revolutionary Guard. Iran may have a nuclear bomb in about ten years, thanks to a negotiated protocol that freed up billions of sanction money and rejuvenated its oil industry, while it goes through the motions of compliance with denuding itself of nuclear capability. China's exponential resurgent growth will overtake the US as world economic power. It will therefore win the third world war without firing a shot. It will control the entire South China Sea and environs, and may swallow Taiwan. As of this writing, I believe we are living in the most dangerous time faced by the benighted human race in its history. As a *National Post* columnist recently observed: "It is a small, inter-related, dangerous world where crises can erupt suddenly." Well, perhaps Elon Musk and Stephen Hawking are wrong in their apprehension of the triumph of artificial intelligence a.k.a. machine learning, and the decline and eventual wipeout of the species known as the human race. Roll on the replicants, provided they can be programmed against violence. Feed them some memories and some artificial emotions, and a better class of species may evolve!

• • •

Thus in my approaching dotage I end every week with my favourite columns from the *National Post* newspaper – somewhat right-wing, like the aging author – and for a more 'liberal' interpretation of world events, and superb coverage, the weekly *The Economist*.

There is time for rumination in retirement. As each long day stretches into night, the aging barrister has time for contemplation, accompanied, say, by the soothing ballades of Gould's interpretations of William Byrd and 16th-century contemporary Orlando Gibbons. One wonders, what is there left 'to shape and sharp one's purpose / to point one's passionate aim…?' On balance, sitting here late at night in front of a roaring fire with single malt and a good cigar to hand, perhaps the legal revolution all innovations considered is positive, but the world revolution is beginning to look like a second hand clunker with bald tires.

My late wife was brought up in her early years in Mufulira, five miles from the Congo border in what was then called Northern Rhodesia. Later a teacher in Southern Rhodesia, she experienced the dramatic upheavals and revolutions that transfigured and transformed modern Africa. It is profoundly interesting – at least to me – that two African tableaux sum up all that was 'bad' and all that was 'good' about the colonial era. Kurtz's "The horror, the horror!" is surely the template today for the wholesale brutal murder, rapine, exploitation, slavery, cruelty, violence and baseness that characterized the colonial polity of the day. But where else can one encounter the day-to-day civility, the comfortable old-boy/old-school network of decent, well-meaning persons, the very personification of courtesy and stability, than in the classic greeting, "Dr. Livingstone, I presume?"

In the course of my late night ruminations, I have cause to reflect upon the human condition. I am reminded of the words of The Grateful Dead: "What a long, strange trip it has been…" Of course, I have been heavily influenced by writers I admire. My books are everything, my only prized possessions.

The inevitable descent upon me of ennui after a life of combat moves me once more to the observations of Dr. George Steiner in *In Bluebeard's Castle*: "Madness, death are preferable to the interminable Sunday and suet of a bourgeois life-form.... What was a gifted man to do after Napoleon?"

Ennui. What was the gifted man to do after fifty years on his feet in courtrooms? One has a desire to be rejuvenated. But the aging body betrays one. It is hard to accept. It is also inevitable.

As I have noted, I read everything and revisit favoured writers, like Kafka and Dostoevsky. Kafka knew a thing or two about the hopeless oppression of faceless law and order. Dostoevsky knew a thing or two about crime and punishment. And he ended his life in the firm belief that "compassion is the chief law of human existence." They could both have taught a thing or two to the late unlamented federal Conservative government, for example, that judges are not rubber stamps handing out legislated mandatory minimum sentences – an "absurd straitjacket" says Conrad Black – but there must be a weighing of mitigating and aggravating factors by a fair and impartial and independent tribunal.

There is a case to be made against simply building more jails. There will be less repeat offenders and we would save a great deal of money if the government replaced knee-jerk imprisonment for non-violent offenders with community service and perhaps half-way houses.

• • •

Every Friday afternoon at 4:30 I meet the members of my old law firm at an agreeable auberge just down the road from the Court-house. We have always stayed in close touch, we practiced together as great friends, and the Friday occasion is one of conviviality. Of seven members of our former criminal law firm, five of them are now judges, currently presiding in various courts: Sheilah Martin, Peter Martin, Earl Wilson, Jim Ogle, and Willie deWit. The only other member besides myself who did not want to go to the Bench is the redoubtable Hersh Wolch QC, also a septuagenarian, who heads up the successor firm and still vigorously defends his clients daily in Court.

My friends at the Bar, well, both bars, our Professional calling and our watering hole, have always showed interest in my writing, which I have appreciated. When I wrote *A Painful Duty*, I was queried about the title and explained that defending the basest and meanest of the realm, as well as the innocent, which was the duty of the barrister, was extraordinarily hard work, and in many ways was painful. After hours of assiduous preparation, sleepless and often exhausted, it was always with trepidation that I marched into Court with that hard knot in my stomach knowing that I would have to put that crucial question to the hostile witness that might win the day. Or kill my case. That was always painful. As was day-to-day practice before sometimes difficult judges on occasion opposed by some learned friends who were neither learned nor friendly.

As to the title of this book; the privilege of witnessing the fifty tumultuous years of the various revolutionary events of change in my Profession was, for the most part, a positive experience, and certainly a lot less painful than slugging it out in the courtroom. However, I cannot conclude that this truly incredible revolution was entirely without pain, because of some of the negative aspects with which I have dealt in this memoir. Without overstating, I particularly regret the passing of the days of intimate camaraderie shared with the members of a smaller Bench and practicing Bar, and what I view as a steep decline in the art and calling of the advocate. Hence "less painful."

INDEX

**Tough Crimes: True Cases by
Top Canadian Criminal Lawyers**

Book One in the True Cases Series
Eds: CD Evans and Lorene Shyba

Tough Crimes is a collection of
thoughtful and insightful essays from
some of Canada's most prominent
criminal lawyers. Stories include
wrongful convictions, reasonable
doubt, homicides, and community.

Price: $29.95 *Trade Paperback*
ISBN: 978-0-9689754-6-6 (2014)

**Shrunk: Crime and Disorders
of the Mind**

Book Two in the True Cases Series
Eds: Drs. Lorene Shyba and J. Thomas Dalby
Foreword: Dr. Lisa Ramshaw

Shrunk is a collection of chapters by
eminent Canadian and international
forensic psychologists and psychia-
trists who write about mental health
issues they face and what they are
doing about it.

Price: $29.95 *Trade Paperback*
ISBN: 978-0-9947352-0-1 (2016)

**More Tough Crimes: True Cases by
Canadian Judges and Criminal Lawyers**

Book Three in the True Cases Series
Eds: William Trudell and Lorene Shyba
Foreword: Hon. Patrick LeSage

More Tough Crimes provides a unique
window into the world of criminal
justice. Many cases are recent,
but some from the past were so
disturbing they resonate in the public
consciousness.

Price: $29.95 *Trade Paperback*
ISBN: 978-09947352-5-6 (2017)

Women in Silks: True Cases by
Canadian Women in Criminal Justice

Upcoming!

Book Four in the True Cases Series
ISBN: 978-0-9947352-4-9

 & Durvile.com

Milt Harradence: The Western Flair

Foreword by Hon. John C. Major, CC QC
Retired Justice, Supreme Court of Canada

"It should find a permanent home in every trial lawyer's library."
— Ron MacIsaac, Lawyers Weekly

In Milt Harradence: The Western Flair, C.D. Evans perpetuates the legend of his flamboyant, larger-than-life colleague with whom he shared thrills, spills, brilliant courtroom spars.

Price: $30.00 *Trade Paperback*
16 pages of colour photos.
ISBN: 978-0-9689754-0-4

A Painful Duty
40 Years at the Criminal Bar

A Memoir by CD Evans
Reflections Series, Book 1

"Very rarely have I read a memoir or autobiography whose author had as overwhelming concern for truth and fairness as Evans displays in this book."
— Alex Rettie, Alberta Views

Evans reveals insights into the practice and the characters of the Criminal Bar, with special tributes to no-nonsense judges.

Price: $42.50 *Trade Paperback*
16 pages of colour photos.
ISBN: 978-0-9689754-3-5

Less Painful Duties
Reflections on the Revolution
in the Legal Profession
by CD Evans
Reflections Series, Book 2

Evans reflects on revolutionary changes that have come about within the Canadian legal profession, in particular the Criminal Bar, over the past fifty years. Topics he covers include ascendancy of women in the profession, effects on criminal litigation of the Canadian Charter of Rights, and the impacts of cell phone and computer technology.

Price: $29.95 *Trade Paperback*
ISBN: 978-0-9952322-1-1

5000 Dead Ducks
Lust and Revolution in the Oilsands

A Novel by C.D. Evans and L.M. Shyba

"5000 Dead Ducks may be a satire, a fever dream of sorts, but its message is clear: When it comes to the oilsands, the stakes are so high that anything is possible."
— Gillian Steward, Toronto Star

A comedy satire about an unscrupulous group of "Candidian" lawyers engineer a revolution to take over the "Alberia" oilsands.

Price: $16.95 *Trade Paperback*
ISBN: 978-0-9689754-4-2

Stop Making Art and Die
Survival Activities for Artists

By Rich Théroux

 UpRoute Imprint

"Stop Making Art and Die asks big questions about creativity, fulfillment, and happiness."
— Eric Volmers, Calgary Herald

The first adult activity book that makes it impossible not to succeed and flourish as and artist by encouraging a deeper understand of art.

Price: $42.50 *Trade Paperback*
ISBN: 978-0-9689754-3-5

A Wake in the Undertow
Rumble House Poems

by Rich Theroux and Jess Szabo

 UpRoute Imprint

Arms flung wide
Rib cages swung open
Hearts thunder
Wild vibrations
Where that river
meets the ocean.

Welcome home.

Price: $16.95 *Trade Paperback*
ISBN: 978-0-9689754-9-7

 **DURVILE** PUBLICATIONS & UpRoute *Books and Media*   Durvile.com